The Kentucky Bicentennial Bookshelf
Sponsored by

KENTUCKY HISTORICAL EVENTS CELEBRATION COMMISSION
KENTUCKY FEDERATION OF WOMEN'S CLUBS

and Contributing Sponsors

AMERICAN FEDERAL SAVINGS & LOAN ASSOCIATION
ARMCO STEEL CORPORATION, ASHLAND WORKS
A. ARNOLD & SON TRANSFER & STORAGE CO., INC. / ASHLAND OIL, INC.
BAILEY MINING COMPANY, BYPRO, KENTUCKY / BEGLEY DRUG COMPANY
J. WINSTON COLEMAN, JR. / CONVENIENT INDUSTRIES OF AMERICA, INC.
IN MEMORY OF MR. AND MRS. J. SHERMAN COOPER BY THEIR CHILDREN
CORNING GLASS WORKS FOUNDATION / MRS. CLORA CORRELL
THE COURIER-JOURNAL AND THE LOUISVILLE TIMES
COVINGTON TRUST & BANKING COMPANY
MR. AND MRS. GEORGE P. CROUNSE / GEORGE E. EVANS, JR.
FARMERS BANK & CAPITAL TRUST COMPANY / FISHER-PRICE TOYS, MURRAY
MARY PAULINE FOX, M.D., IN HONOR OF CHLOE GIFFORD
MARY A. HALL, M.D., IN HONOR OF PAT LEE,
JANICE HALL & AND MARY ANN FAULKNER
OSCAR HORNSBY INC. / OFFICE PRODUCTS DIVISION IBM CORPORATION
JERRY'S RESTAURANTS / ROBERT B. JEWELL
LEE S. JONES / KENTUCKIANA GIRL SCOUT COUNCIL
KENTUCKY BANKERS ASSOCIATION / KENTUCKY COAL ASSOCIATION, INC.
THE KENTUCKY JOCKEY CLUB, INC. / THE LEXINGTON WOMAN'S CLUB
LINCOLN INCOME LIFE INSURANCE COMPANY
LORILLARD A DIVISION OF LOEW'S THEATRES, INC.
METROPOLITAN WOMAN'S CLUB OF LEXINGTON / BETTY HAGGIN MOLLOY
MUTUAL FEDERAL SAVINGS & LOAN ASSOCIATION
NATIONAL INDUSTRIES, INC. / RAND MCNALLY & COMPANY
PHILIP MORRIS, INCORPORATED / MRS. VICTOR SAMS
SHELL OIL COMPANY, LOUISVILLE
SOUTH CENTRAL BELL TELEPHONE COMPANY
SOUTHERN BELLE DAIRY CO. INC.
STANDARD OIL COMPANY (KENTUCKY)
STANDARD PRINTING CO., H. M. KESSLER, PRESIDENT
STATE BANK & TRUST COMPANY, RICHMOND
THOMAS INDUSTRIES INC. / TIP TOP COAL CO., INC.
MARY L. WISS, M.D. / YOUNGER WOMAN'S CLUB OF ST. MATTHEWS

WOMEN
IN KENTUCKY

HELEN DEISS IRVIN

THE UNIVERSITY PRESS OF KENTUCKY

Research for The Kentucky Bicentennial Bookshelf
is assisted by a grant from the
National Endowment for the Humanities.
Views expressed in the Bookshelf do not
necessarily represent those of the Endowment.

Library of Congress Cataloging in Publication Data

Irvin, Helen Deiss.
   Women in Kentucky.

   (The Kentucky Bicentennial bookshelf)
   Bibliography: p.
   1. Women—Kentucky—History.   I. Title.   II. Series.
HQ1438.K4I74   301.41'2'09769   77-92924
ISBN 0-8131-0239-1

· Scholarly publisher for the Commonwealth
serving Berea College, Centre College of Kentucky,
Eastern Kentucky University, The Filson Club,
Georgetown College, Kentucky Historical Society,
Kentucky State University, Morehead State University,
Murray State University, Northern Kentucky University,
Transylvania University, University of Kentucky,
University of Louisville, and Western Kentucky University.

Editorial and Sales Offices: Lexington, Kentucky 40506

Contents

For my grandmother, a strong woman:
BESSIE GRAHAM HALLIDAY DAVENPORT
1865-1947

Preface

Wᴴʏ ᴀ ʙᴏᴏᴋ about women in Kentucky? Because their past has been largely ignored. My thesis is simple: women were there, their lives are worth looking at, and often they contributed more than they are given credit for.

In his *New Viewpoints in American History*, Arthur M. Schlesinger observed:

An examination of the standard histories of the United States and of the history textbooks in use in our schools raises the pertinent question whether women have ever made any contributions to American national progress that are worthy of record. If the silence of the historians is to mean anything, it would appear that one-half of our population have been negligible factors in our country's history.

So it has been, with few exceptions, in Kentucky history. Obviously, a small book dealing with a large subject cannot be comprehensive. Choices had to be made. I tried to make them in such a way as to provide some flavor of these invisible lives.

Acknowledgments

I APPRECIATE THE information and cooperation given me by Laura Kinkead Walton, formerly of Planned Parenthood of Lexington; the late Jean Brandeis Tachau, formerly of the Kentucky Birth Control League, Louisville; Jan Harmon of Planned Parenthood of Lexington; Ida Gorshkin of the Women's Trade Union Studies Program of Cornell University, New York City; Arthur Flandreau, head librarian, Berea College; John May, head librarian, Centre College; S. Cecil Herr Perry, Colonial Dames of America; Ruth Davenport Deiss, United Daughters of the Confederacy, and Caufield and Shook, photographers.

Special thanks go to Roemel Henry, archivist emeritus of Transylvania University; Mary Schwalst, former curator of "Liberty Hall," Frankfort; James C. Anderson and David Horvath, University of Louisville Photographic Archives; William Marshall and Terry Birdwhistell of Special Collections, King Library, University of Kentucky; Florence Shelby Cantrill of Lexington for her valuable information and insight; Professor George C. Wright of the University of Kentucky Department of History for his helpful criticism; and Professors Suzanne and Richard Lowitt for their interest and advice.

1

THE SETTLERS

Whilst young Miss Woods dispatched [the Indian's] *life,
the Old Lady Barrd the Door & kept it shut.*

Journal, 1782

ALTHOUGH WOMEN SETTLERS came to Kentucky to stay
in 1775, they are usually ignored in histories, as if they were
invisible or their lives of little interest. They may be depicted, if at all, as passive and fearful. By these timid qualities they are defined as harbingers of a more "refined civilization"—in contrast to that of the Indians who used Kentucky as a hunting ground. But to learn of a woman migrant
on horseback fording a swift river, one child in her arms and
one hanging on behind her, to find other women improvis-
ing a substitute for flax, defending a fort under siege, or
fighting off Indian attackers, is to see women as active par-
ticipants in the rough, precarious life of the settlements.
Visible or not, "refined" or not, women helped settle the
Kentucky frontier. And in doing so, many showed resourcefulness and courage that are seldom remembered.

Few were as enterprising as Polly Mulhollin, who lived on
the Virginia border. To get to America, the young Irish
woman had indentured herself to a neighbor. After working
out her time of servitude, she was free and on her own. By
"cabin rights," she learned, a settler who built a cabin received a hundred acres of land surrounding it, and Polly
Mulhollin realized that nothing was stipulated about actually living there. Putting on a hunting shirt, trousers, and
moccasins, she took an axe and went to work. She not only

1

built a cabin; she built thirty cabins. At a time when naive pioneers were often cheated out of their hard-won land by sharp operators, Polly Mulhollin got her 3,000 acres and held on to them. When she had time, she married, and eventually had many children and a large clan of descendants.

Polly Mulhollin was a borderer, not a Kentuckian, but the same hunger for land and for a second chance in life soon lured men and women settlers into the future state. After Rebecca Boone and her daughter, Jemima, arrived at Boonesborough on September 8, 1775, becoming the first white women to settle in Kentucky, many more followed over the mountains.

Black women, too, slaves of migrating families, made the long journey. One of the first was Molly Logan, who came with her three young sons and the Benjamin Logan family, arriving at St. Asaph's, near present-day Stanford, on March 8, 1776.

The migration itself would have weeded out all but the hardy. Although a party might start out in wagons, most of the route was fit only for pack animals. Hundreds of miles of walking lay ahead. In packsaddles, one on each side of a horse, small children could ride swaddled in bedding. Babies were carried in their mothers' arms, and those travelers too sick to walk could be carried in litters. Some migrants rode pack animals, but most walked, carrying part of the load.

Rain added to the miseries of the trail. "Scald feet," caused by wet shoes or moccasins, were common and painful. Without wagons, the travelers slept outdoors, the women unloading the packhorses each night and setting up makeshift shelters of blankets. In wet weather, neither bedding nor clothing was ever dry. Babies and small children must have presented special difficulties, for although clothing could be washed in creeks, it could not be dried in a rainy Kentucky spring or fall.

Even at best, the way was beset by hardships. Packhorses often fell when the going was rough, or when some animal alarmed them, they might run away, losing their gear in a creek or among the stalks of a canebrake—the "turrabel Cainbrakes," as one journal calls them. Mosquitoes and ticks were a constant problem. And the farther the migrants went, the more tedious the food seemed. A diet of meat, often without salt, was unsatisfying, and many records mention how much these pioneers missed bread. Most of all, the solitude of the wilderness oppressed them. One account tells us that the silence affected even the dogs. Alone or in small groups, hunters sometimes lost their bearings and even their sanity in the forests. Even a large group of travelers had no protection against this alarming feeling of isolation and vulnerability.

But these difficulties were trivial compared to the threat of Indians or winter. Because Indians were more active in the summer, many parties of immigrants started out in early fall, with the goal of arriving and settling in Kentucky before cold weather came. But if the Indians took their time in heading for winter quarters, immigrants too would delay, hoping that they could avoid both Indians and snow. All knew stories of death and captivity, and on the trail they walked past solitary graves of earlier travelers.

Winter on the journey was dreaded almost as much as Indians. In the bitter winter of 1779-80, cattle froze, sheep died from eating ivy, ice formed in minutes on travelers fording creeks, the Kentucky River froze two feet deep, and buffalo and deer starved in the forests. That winter, a migrating family named Davis was marooned by a creek that rose suddenly in the night. Davis tried to swim for help but drowned. Mrs. Davis and her children had no fire, and during the night they froze to death.

Even immigrants who managed to get to Kentucky had suffered so much from exposure that they fell easy prey to sickness after they arrived. Many persons at Harrodsburg were overcome by pains in the head, back, and chest. Even young men who were thought the strongest of settlers died of exposure. Feet, hands, faces were frostbitten. For water, the settlers melted snow, and for food, they ate horses and cattle that had frozen in the fields. A traveler described conditions in March, 1780, at Logan's Station (St. Asaph's) in central Kentucky:

The effects of the severe winter was now sensibly felt, the earth for so long a time being covered with snow and the water entirely froze, the Cane almost all kiled, the Hogs that were in the Country suffered greatly, being frozen to death, in their beds, the deer likewise not being able to get either water or food, were found dead in great numbers, tirkies dropt dead off their roosts and even the Buffalos died starved to death, the vast increase of people, near three thousand that came into this Country with the prodigious losses they had in their cattle and horses, on their Journey, and the severity of the winter after they got here killing such numbers, all contributed to raise the necessaries of life to a most extravagant price.

In 1781, the largest group ever to migrate from Virginia to Kentucky—between five and six hundred people—was spared the ferocity of Indians but not of weather. Prosperous and prudent, the group—an entire congregation of a Baptist church, with others who joined the party—seemed to have everything: skilled woodsmen as leaders, cows to give milk for the children, spinning wheels, churns, bullet molds, extra clothing, warm bedding. But winter caught them. Rain, snow, sleet soaked their clothes, moccasins, and blankets. Packhorses slipped and fell. Streams ran high and had to be forded, through icy water often chest-high. When the water ran too deep, they had to build rafts, unload the packhorses, swim the horses across, and hope that the rafts, carrying children and possessions, would not turn over.

To cover the thirty miles from the Holston River to Cumberland Gap took these people almost three weeks. Thirty miles in three weeks: no records tell us how many died before they finally reached their goal in Garrard County. Nor do we have records of those who were born on the route, and whether they survived. Of a later winter migration, Bishop Asbury wrote: "How much I have suffered on this journey is known only to God and myself."

Unexpected hardship also lay ahead for another large and

4

well-prepared party of about five hundred, making the long trek in 1784. Robert L. Kincaid tells us that traveling single file, as they had to, the line of immigrants stretched out for almost two miles. Well-equipped as they were, they had no defense against an epidemic of measles that swept through the train, striking almost every family. No matter how sick, they had to keep moving. In this migration as in many others, some women must have realized that in spite of all that they could do, a sickly baby or a frail child would make a fresh grave on the route. The trail to Kentucky was no place for the delicate or fearful, though the women who traveled it are sometimes so described.

Sturdy people, those who survived. In the large migration of 1784, before the measles epidemic, another disaster was narrowly averted. Arriving at the rain-swollen Clinch River in late October, the advance guard of armed men decided that the usual fording place was too dangerous, and they rode upriver, around a bend, to make the crossing. Then the women's party, on horseback and mostly armed with pistols, arrived at the usual ford. Jane Trimble, their leader, seeing guards on the other side of the river and not warned that they had crossed upstream, plunged into the rushing water. In her arms was her baby, Allen, and clinging to her back was her three-year-old, William.

Following her into the cold water was Mrs. William Erwin, who carried with her two small black children, one on either side of her horse, riding in a large wallet or pouch. As the current caught them up, wallet and children were swept from Mrs. Erwin's horse, but a man on shore managed to rescue both children. Her horse was washed against a ledge on the far bank, and as she urged him up the bank, he managed to find a foothold in the rocks.

Jane Trimble's horse was still struggling in the current. Gripping bridle and mane with her right hand, she clung to the baby with her left arm and shouted to William to hold on tight. At last they made it to the opposite bank, where her exhausted horse struggled to shore.

In his farewell speech to this large migration, Colonel

James Knox praised the horsemanship of Mrs. Trimble and the courage of the women. Jane Trimble's children survived the hazards of a frontier childhood, Allen to become governor of Ohio, and the tenacious William to have a distinguished career in the War of 1812.

Compared to these migrations overland, the journey by flatboat seems almost luxurious. Some immigrants made the journey on what were essentially large rafts, poled slowly along, while the travelers fished, taught the children their lessons, and occasionally gave birth. But peaceful as the flatboat sounds, it was highly vulnerable to Indian attack. On the same Clinch River in which Mrs. Trimble, Mrs. Erwin, and the four children nearly drowned, a flatboat fell behind the rest of a flotilla one day in the spring of 1780. Seeing their chance, Indians attacked the straggler. Harriette Simpson Arnow relates that the two young men on board jumped off and ran. Left to defend the boat and themselves, the women aboard put up a fierce fight. In the struggle, while throwing supplies over the side to lighten the boat, a Mrs. Peyton accidentally threw her day-old baby into the Clinch. Despite this misfortune, the women fought off the Indians and survived. A young girl, Nancy Gower, although wounded in the thigh, calmly guided the boat to an escape.

Of those who survived the immigration, some were better equipped than others for the rigors of frontier life. One who flourished naturally there was the vigorous Esther Whitley, who came to Kentucky early, in 1775, when fine land was still plentiful. Esther and her husband, William Whitley, were colorful people, tempered by violence, and cool hands in a crisis. A crack shot, Esther Whitley was depended upon as a defender of Logan's Fort. While other women molded bullets, Esther, along with Jane Manifee, took her place among the riflemen.

Her son related with pride that once when the men at Logan's Fort were holding a shooting match in 1777, William Whitley walked in from hunting or scouting, casually handed his rifle to Esther, and urged her to join the contest.

With her first shot, she beat all previous shots. Although the competition went on until nightfall, no one could beat her, and she took the prize: all the bullets scraped from the target, no insignificant matter in a poor frontier settlement where lead was scarce.

In spite of constant danger from Indians, frontier people did not live cooped up in forts. Chores had to be done, wood and water fetched, animals tended. All this the Indians knew and often caught settlers in the middle of such daily tasks.

On the morning of May 20, 1777, Esther Whitley, Anne Logan, and the Logan family's slave, Molly, went outside the fort to milk the cows. As they knew, Indians were waiting nearby, but milking was at all times a woman's chore. With them went four men with rifles as guards. As the women worked, Indians fired at the party, killing one guard and wounding two others severely. The fourth man and the three women ran for the gate. As she ran, Esther Whitley's hat—a borrowed hat—fell off. She stopped and picked it up before she dashed through the gate. Everything that we know about her life is of a piece with this small act.

On their rich land, the Whitleys built the first brick house in Kentucky, located not far from the fort and called "Sportsman Hill." Always openhanded in entertaining, the Whitleys spent considerable money on liquor for the workmen, apparently to encourage their enthusiasm. When finished, the house possessed some startling features that clearly expressed the powerful and original personalities of its owners.

In white brick in the red brick outside wall were mortared, in large letters, William's initials, "W.W." In the opposite wall, in letters equally large, were placed Esther's, "E.W." Over the fireplace, they ordered carved a tasteful row of large dollar-marks. And as patriots, they arranged for thirteen steps to the second floor, in honor of the original states.

Not only did they construct a secret hiding place for women and children—not that Esther would have deigned to use

7

it—but they also made all of the third floor a ballroom. Thus they were prepared for war or peace.

The Whitleys cleared land for the first racetrack in Kentucky. Because they loathed all things British, they ran the horses counterclockwise instead of clockwise as the English did. But time and again, William interrupted this sport for another that he pursued with zest: Indian-chasing. He became the scourge of Indian marauders who raided solitary cabins or attacked the steady stream of immigrants pouring overland into Kentucky.

In October of 1784, we find Esther Whitley as unruffled as ever. When a runner brought her news that a party had been atttacked near Skaggs Creek, William was not at home. Dispatching a servant for him, she picked up a hunting horn and blew loud blasts on it to call the men in from the fields. By the time William got home, Esther had rounded up twenty-one men to go with him, and off they went, thus becoming involved in an adventure with the McClure family, Kentucky settlers who were the Whitleys' polar opposites.

After riding a day and a night, Whitley and his followers caught up with the Indian raiders and overpowered them, rescuing Mrs. McClure and a black woman, whose name is not recorded. Mrs. McClure told her story. When the Indians attacked in the night, her husband ran away into the forest, making no effort to defend the family. Although she and the four children managed to hide, the baby began to cry, and the Indians easily found them. Killing and scalping three of the children, the Indians took her, with the baby, into their camp. The next morning they forced her to mount a wild horse, which threw her. Next they tied her on, as a form of entertainment, and watched as the horse ran through the forest, dashing her against branches as it did so. After that, they stretched the children's scalps to dry and forced the injured woman to do the cooking in sight of them.

Hearing all this, Whitley was incensed at McClure's cowardice. He took Mrs. McClure and her baby back with him to "Sportsman Hill." Offering their hospitality, the Whitleys insisted that she never live with McClure again. But when he turned up, she meekly went back to him, much to the disgust of the Whitleys.

Long after the supply of Indian marauders was exhausted in Kentucky, Whitley got another chance to fight. At the advanced age of 64, he enlisted as a private in the War of 1812, possibly killed Tecumseh, and certainly was killed himself. A sentimentalist, he had asked that his scalp be returned to Esther in Kentucky, but his request was not carried out, and she was deprived of this last memento of their colorful frontier partnership.

Other Kentucky women settlers were well able to contend with the hazards of primitive living and Indian menace. An isolated cabin in Nelson County was the scene of a fierce struggle on a summer night in 1787. About midnight, John Merril heard the family dog barking, and got up uneasily and opened the door. Immediately he was hit by rifle fire, and he fell to the floor, his arm and thigh both broken. Mrs. Merril ran to bolt the door, but the Indians battered it with their tomahawks, quickly chopping a large hole. Casting about for a weapon, Mrs. Merril found only an axe at hand, but with it, John A. M'Clung tells us, she proved "a perfect Amazon both in strength and courage," and she proceeded to kill or badly wound four Indians in turn.

Giving up on the door, the attackers climbed to the roof, intending to drop down the chimney. But Mrs. Merril heard them, and she quickly ripped up the feather bed and threw the feathers onto the coals in the fireplace. Dense smoke and flames poured up the chimney. Half overcome, two Indians fell down onto the hearth and lay dazed in the fire. Before they revived, Mrs. Merril killed them both with the axe. Then, hearing a noise at the door, she turned to find another Indian, the last remaining intact, trying to get in. She struck him a swift blow with the axe, laying open a gash down his cheek, and he ran howling for the woods. Long after, a former prisoner of the Indians reported that in Chillicothe, he had seen this scarred Indian, who "gave an exaggerated account of the fierceness, strength, and courage of the 'long knife squaw.' "

At another cabin, this one in central Kentucky, far from the nearest station, a family named Woods was the target of a sudden Indian raid in the middle of the day. In the summer of 1782, as Mrs. Woods was milking, she saw several Indians moving on her cabin. The only persons at home were a crippled slave and the young Woods daughter, Hannah.

Shouting the alarm, Mrs. Woods ran for the cabin, trying to get inside before the Indians could. But before she could get the door closed, one Indian had forced his way in. While Mrs. Woods struggled to keep the door closed against the other Indians, the black man threw himself on the Indian and the two fell to the floor. As they fought, young Hannah seized an axe and struck the Indian repeated blows, finally killing him. As a contemporary journal put it, "Whilst young Miss Woods dispatched his life, the Old Lady Barrd the Door & kept it shut."

At this point, the slave urged Mrs. Woods to let the Indians in one at a time, so that he and Hannah could kill them individually. Whether this strategy would have worked we do not know, for just then they heard rifle fire. A party of settlers happened to see and follow the Indians, and the embattled householders were rescued.

Arnow tells of an instance down on the Cumberland when Indians caught a small girl, Polly Dunham, outside her cabin and quickly made a thin circular cut around her head, preparing to scalp her. Hearing her screams, her mother snatched up a hoe and ran to defend the child. As the furious woman bore down on them with the hoe, the Indians dropped Polly in amazement and turned their knives on the mother. They wounded her badly, but she fought them off and saved her daughter.

Often, however, these struggles did not have happy endings. We hear of a woman and her two daughters, attacked by twenty-five Wyandots near Estill's Station in central

Kentucky in 1782. They were raped, tomahawked, and scalped, but their names are not remembered.

Much more is known about the terrible night of April 11, 1787, at the home of the Widow Scraggs in Bourbon County. Her cabin was a double one—two rooms, each with a separate door to the outside. In one room the widow lived with her two grown sons, her widowed daughter, and the daughter's baby. In the other room lived two unmarried daughters in their late teens and a little girl, apparently another daughter.

At about eleven o'clock, the family had all gone to bed except for one of the sons, and in the other cabin, one of the daughters, who was weaving. For an hour or so, the son had noticed owl calls, and he had also heard sounds of agitation among the horses—snorting, restless movements.

Suddenly, there were several loud knocks at the door, and a voice said, "Who keeps house?" This greeting was an ordinary one, and it was spoken in good English. Further, the worst of the Indian warfare had been over for some time. The young man went to the door to draw aside the bar. But his mother, the Widow Scraggs, was a frontier veteran, and suddenly sensing that the visitors were Indians, she called to her son not to open the door. As the Indians pounded on the door, the two brothers shot at them, until the attackers moved to the door of the other room of the cabin, a point at which the brothers could not bring their rifles to bear. Picking up some rails from the fence, the attackers battered down the door and seized one of the older daughters. In a brief struggle, the other daughter stabbed one Indian with a knife before being tomahawked, giving the little girl time to get away.

The child ran into the yard, but instead of escaping into the woods, she ran around the house in terror, screaming that her sister was killed. The brothers rushed to the door. Then Mrs. Scraggs made a grim decision. Throwing herself in front of the door, she told her sons—calmly, the records say—not to try to rescue the child, because they would only sacrifice everyone without being able to save her. At that point a scream came from the little girl, then a few moans, and then silence. In a few minutes more they heard the crackling of flames. The Indians had set the adjoining cabin room afire, and soon the whole place was ablaze.

Opening the door, the Widow Scraggs and one of her sons ran in one direction; the daughter, carrying the baby, and the other son ran in another. As Mrs. Scraggs climbed the stile, she was shot several times by the Indians and fell dead. Her son dashed into the woods and escaped, while the other brother fought off the Indians long enough for his sister to get away with the baby. Then he, too, was killed. Taking the remaining sister with them, the Indians ran off.

A light snow had fallen, and a search party that included the surviving brother went out to track down the raiders. Unfortunately they brought along a hound whose baying told the Indians that they were closely pursued. Apparently, too, the captive girl's strength was flagging, and the Indians tomahawked her, leaving her dying for the searchers to find.

Of the family of eight, three managed to survive. So ends the story of the Widow Scraggs and her children: victims but not helpless victims, for their courage and character are obvious.

Frontier stories frequently describe battles with Indians in which women, usually in the dark, loaded rifles, and put out fires in blockhouses or cabins. Like Esther Whitley and Jane Manifee at Logan's Fort, many women could also use a gun. Of the siege of Boonesborough in September, 1778, George W. Ranck says that although only men are counted as defenders of the fort, "women should have been reckoned in—they certainly deserved to be—for in courage and marksmanship they were not to be despised." He mentions, too, a Mrs. Duree, who lived in a cabin near Boonesborough in 1781, and who "took the place of her fallen husband and defended the living and dead in her cabin."

The conduct of women during the siege of Bryant's (or Bryan's) Station, near Lexington, is often described. While hundreds of Indians lay in ambush, the women of the fort agreed to walk down to the creek—the fort having been built, unwisely, at some distance from water—to bring back buckets of water, as they did every day. The purpose was not only to get badly needed water but also to convince the Indians that the settlers did not realize the size of the ambush. Walking into close range of the Indian rifles, the women filled the buckets routinely and carried them back calmly. This act of courage is described by M'Clung in somewhat denigrative terms when he says the defenders hoped "that they [the Indians] would not unmask themselves for the sake of firing at a few women." And typically, he imagines that the yells of the Indians "struck terror to the hearts of women and children, and startled even the men."

Whether their courage is appreciated or not, the Kentucky frontier had its share of self-sufficient women. As William Elsey Connelley observed in 1910:

The division of labor was not so distinct as it is now. Women often worked in the field, plied the axe, sheared the sheep, pulled the flax, plucked the feathers from the geese and ducks and frequently did effective service with the rifle. These things were in addition to their ordinary work of preparing food, spinning and dyeing thread and yarn, weaving cloth therefrom, making the clothing, and attending to many other affairs amid all the care and anxieties incident to rearing large families on an exposed and dangerous frontier.

When Ann Kennedy Wilson Poague Lindsay McGinty—frequently widowed by frontier hazards—settled in Kentucky in 1775, she brought with her a spinning wheel, said to be the first in the future state. And when she moved to Harrodsburg in February, 1776, she began to think of ways to solve an urgent problem among the settlers there: a shortage of warm clothing. What small planting area they cleared was used for corn, for food took precedence over flax. Yet they needed clothing immediately. Experimenting with the fibers of "nettles and other weeds," according to her daughter, she arrived at an acceptable substitute for flax.

With her children, she ventured out of Fort Harrod to gather nettles, and weighed the weeds down with stones in the creek, to let the water rot off the outer stalk. Later she "spread, rotted, broke, swingled, and hacked" the weeds, twisting together several strands of fiber, and she used these strands to weave a frail fabric on a home-built loom. Further experiment led her to interweave her nettle-thread with buffalo wool, producing "linsey-woolsey." This strong, warm material was soon in general use, flax replacing nettles as soon as it could be raised.

While these experiments were carried on by Ann Kennedy, another Harrodsburg woman, Jane Coomes, was organizing the settlement children into a rudimentary school, the first in Kentucky. In 1776, with the menace of Indian warfare close at hand, and without books except for an arithmetic she transcribed, she began to teach Kentucky's new population of children. By 1790, two hundred small outpost schools existed in the future state.

Some women came to Kentucky on their own. In addition to widows who headed families, "many young unmarried women . . . had ventured to risk themselves in Kentucky" by 1781, according to M'Clung. Referring to them, typically, as if they were some sort of commodity, he says that they "were disposed of very rapidly to the young hunters."

A few women disposed of themselves, however, going into business on their own. One of these was Molly Davis, who owned a tavern near Cumberland Gap, near the present site of Middlesboro. Although Moses Austin, father of Stephen Austin, was favorably impressed by very little on his journey to Kentucky in 1796, he had nothing but praise for Molly Davis:

We took our leave of Mrs Davis, who I must take the liberty to say may be Justly call Capn Molly of Cumberland Mountain, for she Fully Commands this passage to the New World. She soon took the freedom to tell me she was a Come by chance her mother she knew little of and her Father less. as to herself she said pleasure was the onely thing she had in View; and that She had her Ideas of life and its injoyments.

Much earlier, Daniel Smith was not so pleased with another woman, making her living as a landlady in frontier Kentucky. She was "a Xantippe," he said, and dirty to boot.

Certainly women of all sorts made an impact on frontier life. Of the arrival of women in Boonesborough, a recent account concludes: "The women not only exerted a certain refining influence in the crude backwoods fortress but they symbolized the arrival of civilization on the banks of the Kentucky." In their own time, some observers had reservations about the refined and civilized qualities of the early women settlers. As a captive in 1779, Lord Henry Hamilton said of Logan's Station: "The people here were not exceedingly well disposed to us and we were accosted by the females especially in pretty coarse terms. But the Captain [Logan] and his wife . . . were very civil and tractable." One of those women who accosted Hamilton was the sharp-shooting Jane Manifee, who picked up a tomahawk Hamilton had with him and remarked that the weapon must have been used on women and children. Turning on him, she threatened to kill him with the same tomahawk—creating an awkward frontier social situation for their hosts.

The settlers may have been at their worst with Hamilton; they called him the "Hair-Buyer" and believed that he incited the Indians to excesses. But a more neutral figure, Colonel William Fleming, who traveled in Kentucky in the winter of 1779-80, came not as a captive enemy but as chairman of a commission to settle land disputes—yet he, too, did not think much of the arrival of civilization in Kentucky.

A physician, Fleming observed of Harrodsburg:

The Spring at this place is below the fort and fed by ponds above the Fort so that the whole dirt and filth . . . putrified flesh, dead dogs, horse, cow, hog excrements and human odour all wash into the spring which with the Ashes and sweepings of filthy cabbins, the dirtiness of the people, steeping skins to dress and washing every sort of dirty rags and cloths in the spring perfectly poisons the water and makes the most filthy nauseous potation of the water imaginable.

Much later, Moses Austin noted that eighteen families had settled along the road from Cumberland Gap to Crab Orchard, and in his opinion, every one of them "appeared to be little removed from savages in their manners or morals." Further, the new settlers following the pioneers into Kentucky were a sorry lot, he thought. Austin observed that many of them, in the depth of winter, were barefoot, scarcely clothed, paupers with neither money nor provisions. Swarming into Kentucky, they seemed to him destined "to become hewers of wood and Drawers of water."

The recollections of a woman who lived in Harrodsburg in its earliest days indicate that the fort was a rough-and-ready settlement. As an old woman, Elizabeth Poague Thomas—daughter of Ann Kennedy, the cloth-maker—recalled settling in Harrodsburg when she was eleven years old. Her story is one of constant danger from Indians, scalpings, stabbings, shootings, sudden violence often unexpectedly flaring up during daily chores, while letting the pigs out, getting the wood.

Mrs. Thomas told "an amusing anecdote" about an Irishman, Edward Worthington, and his "wife or rather a woman by the name of Betsy with whom he lived as such." When Worthington marched with George Rogers Clark in the Vincennes campaign in 1778, he left Betsy in Harrodsburg. Before long, she took up with Evan Shelby, Jr., "who had a sham marriage with her which she insisted was good and it cost him some trouble and money to get clear of her." He succeeded, however, and she rejoined Worthington and lived several more years with him in Harrodsburg. The relaxed view that the community took of Betsy, and the entertainment it found in Shelby's efforts to get rid of her, indicate no very stringent standards of behavior.

Indicative too, of the level of "refinement" in the settlement is a small incident that took place in 1776. Notes of Mrs. Thomas's account tell us: "Next morning the fight, when Ben. Linn killed [and scalped] the Indian, and McGary w'd. This dead Indian was brought to the Fort for the women and children to look at, and then dragged him off and buried him." These ragtag women and children, gathering fascinated around the Indian's mutilated body on a summer's day, must have mirrored almost identical scenes in Indian villages.

To say that Kentucky's women settlers exerted a refining influence "and symbolized the arrival of civilization" in the future state is chivalrous, but perhaps sentimental veneration. What can be said of them is that they were strong, or they could not have survived, and that many had remarkable courage and resourcefulness as well.

It seems enough.

2

THE CAPTIVES

Before her marriage she had killed bears, wolves, panthers and other wild animals.
Said of Jenny Wiley (1760-1831) by her son

Women had lived among the ancient, vanished peoples whose bones and possessions were turned up by plows when Kentucky became farmlands. And although by the time settlers arrived, Kentucky was not a permanent home for Indians, nevertheless Cherokee, Shawnee, Wyandot, Chickasaw and others, men and women, crossed the future state, hunting and traveling, and living there from time to time.

Of the Indian women, accounts vary and are often inconsistent. Some find them praiseworthy. According to Arnow, unlike the wives of white settlers, Indian women were represented in their councils. When Richard Henderson traded goods for lands that the Cherokee used for hunting, a Cherokee woman was present, serving as envoy for the women of the tribe. And in Chickasaw councils "six beloved old women" were allowed in each temple. Speaking highly of the Chickasaw, the Atkin Report of 1775 added: "Even their Women handle Arms, and face an Enemy like Men."

But no romantic ideas of egalitarianism are passed along by Colonel James Smith. A prisoner of the Indians from 1755 to 1759, Smith eventually settled in Bourbon County. As he recalled his Indian captors, "The lives of the men are passed in alternate actions of the most violent kind, and indolence the most excessive. . . . War and hunting are their only serious occupations, and all the drudgery of life devolves upon the squaws." When Smith once joined the women in hoeing corn, the Indians rebuked him, "observing, that it was degrading to a warrior to be engaged in labor like a squaw."

Physically powerful, Indian women could travel as fast as a horse, Smith reported, and pack heavy loads. Once when carrying a piece of buffalo for two or three miles, Smith was exhausted, but "One of the squaws laughed heartily, and coming up, relieved him of a large part of it, adding it to her own pack, which before was equal to [his]."

In an account Smith gave of a domestic quarrel, no great submissiveness is shown by an Indian wife. Indians were well known for their permissive child-rearing, but on this occasion, an Indian stepfather took a whip of buffalo hide to one of his stepsons. Hearing the boy yell, his mother, a Wyandot, intervened angrily, telling her husband that the child was no slave to be whipped and that a ducking in the creek would be ample punishment. The stepfather listened calmly, lit his pipe, and strolled off. But the mother was not appeased. Catching a horse, she loaded her children on it and set off for a Wyandot village forty miles away. Eventually her husband had to ride there to make peace with his wife for his offense to her child.

Accounts of the demeanor of Indian women vary with the reporter. One early traveler noted that "The Cherokee women are elegantly formed, have sprightly eyes, accompanied with modesty and chastity, which renders them far from uninteresting objects." But Smith found them otherwise. Enjoying liquor and revelry as much as did the Indian men, the women were the sexual aggressors, or so Smith claimed:

With them, all coyness, reserve, and pretty delays are confined to the gentlemen. The young squaws are bold, forward, and by no means delicate in urging their passion; and a particularly handsome or promising young hunter, is often reduced to desperate extremities, to escape the toils of these female Lotharios!

19

Sentimentality in one report, or tall tale in the other? One cannot be certain.

Between whites and Indians, relationships were usually violent, bristling with brutality on both sides. Nevertheless, Elizabeth Poague Thomas, who came to Kentucky as a child in 1775, recalled a small celebration of community and innocence on the Wilderness Road. Notes of her account tell us: "on the way 10 Cherokees and a squaw came up to Calloway and Poague's and were friendly and talked—near Cm'd [Cumberland] river; after they left they killed a small buffalo, and divided with the whites." Even though this incident took place before the great tide of migrants began pouring into Kentucky, it was unusual. Early, the Indians understood that immigration would despoil their rich hunting lands, and their hostility was well founded.

During the relatively brief period when Indians and newly arrived settlers lived in proximity in Kentucky, an almost mythic fear of miscegenation haunted the frontier. Like the similar fear that would be directed in the next century toward blacks, this attitude did not apply to white men and Indian women, as it would not extend to white slaveholders and their black women slaves. The mixing of races in itself was not the issue; what was forbidden was the white woman's part in doing so.

As for white men and Indian women, trappers often arrived at fur-trading centers accompanied by Indian wives, proudly decked in finery. Even a formal marriage was not forbidden. The Atkin Report of 1775 urged that soldiers garrisoned in Indian country be encouraged to marry Indian wives, "the Breed proving the hardiest and best attached." Further, the report proposed that convicts be sent to far-off forts to plant corn for Indians: "And by marrying Indian wives . . . they will strengthen the place, & their Offspring prove a valuable sort of Inhabitants."

But the union of white women and Indian men was a different matter. This prohibition may have stemmed in part from the view that women were property, not to be shared, involuntarily or voluntarily. And possibly Indians, like blacks, were perceived as close to nature, possessing a primitive power, a superior vitality that threatened white males.

Whatever the cause, there is evidence that white women captives who returned home were devalued, objects of gossip and a kind of ostracism or unspoken disapproval, as if suspected of cohabiting with the enemy. Some experienced melancholy, perhaps because they had survived and others, often their own children, had not. Perhaps, too, their neighbors were uneasy around them. The end of their captivity was not the end of their ordeal.

Twenty years before the Boone women settled in Kentucky, another woman wandered through the Kentucky forests. She was a captive, the earliest known in the future state. Mary Draper Ingles had been seized with her two small sons and her sister-in-law in a raid on the back settlements of Virginia, July 8, 1755. She was no ordinary woman, as Robert L. Kincaid describes her: "Strong and athletic, she could turn her hand to any job with the best of men, could ride, shoot, cut wood, work in the fields and do all the heavy labor required of rugged life on the frontier." Although some captives became habituated to Indian life in the months or years spent with the tribes, Mary Draper Ingles never stopped looking for a chance to escape.

North of the Ohio, the Ingles captives were separated. The little boys—Thomas, four, and George, two—were taken to Detroit, and the sister-in-law to Chillicothe to join the family of a chief. To add to her distress, Mary Draper Ingles, pregnant with her third child, went into labor. In the night she gave birth to a daughter. Knowing that if she could not keep pace with the Indians, she and the baby would be killed, the next morning she mounted a horse, the baby in her arms, and rode on with her captors.

Three months after the raid, the Indians traveled to Kentucky to make salt at Big Bone Lick, in what later became Boone County. While working at this chore without a guard, Mrs. Ingles and another captive, usually called "an old Dutch [or German] woman," decided to escape. But that decision implied another, harder one. Unable to travel quickly through a strange wilderness with a baby, Mrs. Ingles was forced to leave the child with the Indians. She never heard of the baby again.

Following the south bank of the Ohio, the two women moved as rapidly as possible through creeks, swamps, and the dreaded canebrakes, living on whatever they could find: berries, bark, roots, some Indian corn. After weeks of hunger and exhaustion, the old Dutch woman lost her mind. That was not an uncommon occurrence. In the silence of the forests, even experienced and well-nourished hunters sometimes lost their sanity.

Now Mary Ingles had to contend not only with the wilderness, wild animals, hunger, fatigue, swollen feet, and pursuing Indians, but also with a companion who was raving mad, threatening to kill and eat her. To gain time, Mrs. Ingles told her that they would draw straws to see who ate whom. The demented old woman won and flung herself on the younger woman. They fought until Mrs. Ingles could tear herself away and run into the forest.

In a remarkable exhibition of woodsmanship, after forty days Mary Ingles arrived at a cabin fifteen miles from her home. A search party found the old woman as well. Resourceful even in her madness, she had found a hunter's camp and some food and had caught a stray horse. Even without the search party, she would soon have reached the settlements. With food and rest, her mind cleared, and she was delighted to see Mary Ingles again. Later she joined a party headed through the Shenandoah toward her home in Pennsylvania. Whether she made it, and even who she was, we do not know.

Five years later, Mrs. Ingles's brother got word of his missing wife and ransomed her. She was able to tell the family that George, the younger child, had died soon after being separated from his mother. She knew nothing of Thomas. Although Mrs. Ingles had three more daughters and a son, she always hoped for word of Thomas. And at age seventeen he was found, living with the Shawnee. An Indian in language, habits, and attitudes, Thomas did not want to return, but he eventually did so. Thus Mary Ingles got back one of her missing children, though his very strangeness was a reminder that the Indians and the wilderness had changed her life forever.

Brief references to other captives tell us little of their experiences. M'Clung mentions that in 1780, a "Mrs. Dunlap, of Fayette, who had been several months a prisoner amongst the Indians on Mad River, made her escape, and returned to Lexington." How she accomplished that, we are not told. Among the large Baptist migration from Virginia, one family fell prey to Indians after arriving safely and settling in central Kentucky. Miles Hart was killed; Mrs. Hart and their children were dragged off to a captivity of five years before their eventual ransom. And M'Clung gives us a glimpse of a grim scene in describing the captivity of Simon Kenton:

He sat silent and dejected upon the floor of the cabin, awaiting the moment which was to deliver him to the stake, when the door of the council house opened, and Simon Girty, James Girty, John Ward, and an Indian, came in with a woman (Mrs. Mary Kennedy) as a prisoner, together with seven children and seven scalps.

Not all captives were white. Kincaid says that Indians

on October 6, 1774 captured a Negro woman near Shelby's Fort [on the Virginia border] and tortured her in an effort to get her to tell the number of men and guns in the stockade. She managed to escape and reported that one of the men appeared whiter than the rest and could speak good English.

A short but famous captivity is that of Daniel Boone's daughter, Jemima, and her two friends, Betsy and Frances Callaway, in July of 1776. They had paddled a canoe across the Kentucky River and were seized by four Shawnee on the far bank. During the night, search parties led by their fathers tracked them down near Blue Licks and rescued them.

And that summer at Harrodsburg, in what Elizabeth Poague Thomas believed was the first wedding in Kentucky, the bride was a former captive. With her mother and brother, Hannah Sovereigns had been held captive for six years. The Shawnee had cut out the older woman's tongue, but although she could not speak, she survived. Whether Hannah Sovereigns's value was diminished by her captivity is moot: the bridegroom was Ben Linn, who had lived for years among the Indians and was fluent in four Indian languages. No stranger to Indian ways, it was he who killed and scalped the Indian whose mutilated body was dragged into Fort Harrod. Hannah Sovereigns's captivity would not necessarily have devalued her to such a man.

Kentucky's best-known Indian captive is, of course, Jenny (or Jennie) Wiley, born Jean Sellards on the Virginia border. Accounts, even current ones, of Jenny Wiley usually emphasize only her appearance: dark-haired, handsome, "of fine form." But like Mary Draper Ingles, she was no helpless captive, passively awaiting a doubtful rescue. Her son, Adam, and others who knew her described Jenny Sellards in other terms, as William Elsey Connelley tells us:

All agree that she was strong and capable of great exertion and great endurance. Until past middle life she was of fine form and her movements were quick. . . . Her eyes were black. She was above medium height. Her face was agreeable and indicated superior intelligence. She was persistent and determined in any matter she had decided to accomplish. She labored in her father's fields. She was familiar with every feature of woodcraft and was a splendid shot with the rifle; even after she settled in the Big Sandy Valley it required an expert to equal her. Before her marriage she had killed bears, wolves, panthers and other wild animals. She was at home in the woods and could hold her way over the trails of the country either by day or by night. She was endowed with an abundance of good hard Scotch common sense. In spinning, weaving, and other work of the household she was proficient. I have set down what her son said about her. Most of it was confirmed by

24

other witnesses. Her son insisted that until age began to tell on her she was a handsome woman.

In short, a powerful wilderness woman.

At age twenty-nine, Jenny Wiley lived on the border with her husband, Thomas, an Irish immigrant, and her four children, the youngest fifteen months old. Their cabin was near that of Matthias Harman on Walker's Creek. A relentless enemy of all Indians, the fanatical Harman had recently killed the son of a Cherokee chief.

On an October afternoon in 1789, mistaking the Wiley cabin for Harman's, eleven Indians burst through the Wileys' front door. Killing and scalping the three older children and Mrs. Wiley's young brother, they took her captive. Now the property of a Shawnee chief, she was hurried into the woods in the pouring rain, carrying her youngest child. Her dog followed hesitantly at a distance.

A fifteen-month-old child is a heavy burden, and Jenny Wiley was also far advanced in pregnancy. But she knew that if she could not keep up with the Indians, who sped along the trail unburdened, they would kill the child. Fearing pursuit, the Indians stopped that night only for a quick meal of venison, and then rushed on for the rest of the night and all of the following day, making no stop until late afternoon. That night she watched the Indians—a mixed band of Cherokee, Shawnee, Wyandot, and Delaware—make hoops of green branches. On these they stretched the scalps of her three other children and her brother.

For four days she managed to stagger along with the child, struggling through thickets and swollen creeks, drawing on reserves of strength while the child—whether boy or girl is not known—screamed and cried until it was hoarse. But at last, she fell behind. The Cherokee chief seized the child by the feet and swung it against a tree, dashing out its brains. He paused briefly to take the scalp, and the band hurried along.

On the ninth day, they reached the Ohio, where the group divided, five taking Mrs. Wiley up the Little Sandy

River. There she went into labor. Afraid that the Indians would kill her if she delayed them, she concealed her condition as long as possible and continued along the march. At last, birth was imminent, and there was no hiding the fact. Making camp, the Indians put her into a rockhouse and left her alone. She delivered her own child, a boy.

A rockhouse is only an overhanging rock, not a cave, but Jenny Wiley survived the winter there because of an unusual spell of good weather. The Indians brought her meat, and she gathered her own firewood. A hardy child, the baby also survived the cold, only to perish in an Indian test of manhood. Testing him by floating him out on a stream tied to a piece of dry bark, the Indians tomahawked him when he cried. Thus Jenny Wiley saw her fifth child killed and scalped.

In the spring, the Indians moved on to a buffalo lick, where she was forced to perform all of the drudgery of the camp. Gutting and skinning animals they killed, she also cared for the pelts. She planted corn, gathered wood, did the cooking, and carried ore from a nearby lead mine. To smelt the lead for bullets, she had to collect large stacks of wood and maintain a hot fire for hours. Meanwhile, the warriors hunted occasionally, spending most of the time lounging or sleeping in a rockhouse.

Intelligent as she was, Mrs. Wiley picked up Shawnee and a little of several other Indian languages. She learned that the Shawnee chief planned to take her deep into Indian country beyond the Ohio. Through the summer and early fall, she worked on and waited for a chance to escape.

Toward the end of October, the Indians brought in a young white man and tortured him at the stake. In a frenzy, they turned to their other captive, and tying her to a tree, they told her that they would burn her. Facing such a death, Jenny Wiley was composed, almost contemptuous. Perhaps because of her courage, the Cherokee chief stopped the execution.

But more trouble lay ahead. An enemy throughout her

captivity, the Cherokee had always treated her badly, and now he bought her from the Shawnee chief. His first act was to tie her up painfully with raw buffalo thongs. Some versions of her story have it that the Cherokee told her she was to go with him to his town on the Little Tennessee, and there she was to teach his wives how to write and to weave cloth. Since she was most likely illiterate, perhaps that is a bit of embroidery designed to improve her status. Other accounts said that she was to be one of his wives—a prospect that her son, in later years, did not care to contemplate.

That night, still painfully bound, Jenny Wiley dreamed that the young man who died under torture that day appeared, pointing the way to a fort built by settlers. She awoke believing that the time had come to escape. Perhaps her brush with death that day made her less afraid. The next day, while the Indians hunted, a heavy rainstorm blew up. She managed to roll along the ground until she lay in a puddle of water, soaking her rawhide bonds so that she could slip them off her hands and feet. Then, picking up a tomahawk and a knife, she ran to the creek and began wading downstream to avoid leaving a trail.

Her dog was still with her. One version of her story tells that she tied him to a big stone to keep him from following her. Another claims that the dog came after her, running along the banks of the creek (one says in freshly fallen snow) instead of through the water. To keep her trail concealed, she was forced to kill him, holding his head under water until he drowned.

For eighteen hours she waded in overflowing streams, often against swift currents, convinced that her captors were close behind. At dawn, on the other bank of the river, she saw the fort that appeared in her dream. Managing to persuade its occupants to help her across on a raft, she entered the fort just as the Indians appeared from the woods. With them, say some stories, was her dog. The Cherokee chief shouted that he had paid for her and had saved her life. "Honor, Jenny, honor!" he is supposed to

27

have called. (Or alternatively, "Whoopee, my pretty Jinny!") At length they turned back into the forest, followed by the dog.

They continued to prowl around the fort for several weeks. When winter came on, Matthias Harman, the Indian fighter, and a party of men took her back to Virginia to her husband and kin. Along the way, the Indians attacked the group on several occasions. Connelley says that "Mrs. Wiley had to bear a rifle and fight with the others, which she did effectively and with a good will."

What happened to Jenny Wiley? She and her husband lived in Virginia for about twelve years. Then they settled in Kentucky, in the Big Sandy country, near where she had been held captive. They had five more children, three sons and two daughters. Thomas died in 1810, and Jenny in 1831, at seventy-one, a remarkable age for those times. Their descendants lived on, a large clan, near the Big Sandy.

After Jenny Wiley returned from captivity, gossip circulated that she had given birth to an Indian child, a daughter. Her son, Adam, later denied this story vigorously, just as he denied the story that she was to be one of the Cherokee's wives. Some even claimed that Adam himself was half-Indian, because he had dark skin and black hair, like his mother's. Since Adam Wiley was not born until 1798, that rumor was clearly untrue. But the extent of this gossip indicates the fear of miscegenation that pervaded the frontier.

The Kentucky novelist, Elizabeth Madox Roberts, deals with this phenomenon in her novel of Kentucky pioneer life, *The Great Meadow*. Her protagonist, a young woman named Diony, speaks:

"We live at the very inside of war, in the middle and midst of hate and kill. There's blood on every side of us. Every man I could name in the fort has had one killed, a brother or a father or a child, a sister or a wife carried away. Martin Wilson's wife, up on the Kanawha, found her own way back home after two years gone, came back with the Indian baby she had two months later. . . . And Martin Wilson can't go back to his home because he can't mend his hate for this little Indian child his wife, Lettie, has got in their cradle, her own baby that she pities and holds in her arms. He can't find his way in so much trouble, his hate torn in two."

The melancholy of the returned captive is another phenomenon that the novelist addresses. Neighbors gossip about one such woman:

the Tolliver woman was thin and broken and covered over with sadness . . . which was forever present in her abstracted and dull face. . . .
"Who speaks back to Sallie Tolliver when she mutters on the stairs?"
"It's because she's been far into the wilderness. . . ."
"She talks to Indians."
"She talks to scalps, maybe. Old scalps, dry and withered."
"To far-off places she remembers."
"She talks to the dead."

But Sallie never speaks of what she has seen. Much later, on the Kentucky frontier, one of their number is carried off by Indians. That night memories are shared:

Women huddled near a fire in a cabin told fearful stories of captives.
"Made her walk every step of the way, and made her carry around her neck the bloody scalps of her own children, tied around her own throat. . . ."
A woman sitting by the corner of the hearth spoke then. She had been a captive in Tennessee. Another had seen a fearful thing in the Kanawha country. They were Sallie Tollivers whose tongues were let go for a season, the first woman bearing a strange likeness to the Tolliver woman . . . the same bleared eyes, the same abstracted gaze. . . . The woman lit her pipe with a coal of fire, picking the coal lightly out of the ashes with her bare hand. She told a story of plunder and rapine, her cabin burned, her children killed while they ran to hide. Then she dropped the pipe to the hearth out of her hand that had suddenly lost its strength, and she began to call each child by name.

29

In his journal, Lord Henry Hamilton wrote of Mary Draper Ingles, whom he met twenty years after her captivity. A man who was accused of paying Indians for scalps and captives, he noted of Mrs. Ingles that "terror and distress had left so deep an impression on her mind that she appeared absorbed in a deep melancholy, and left the arrangement of household concerns & the reception of strangers to her lovely daughters."

Although Indians and settlers lived in proximity only briefly in Kentucky, women who had the misfortune to fall into the enemy's hands paid a heavy price. What Indian women experienced we do not know. But white women escaped physical suffering inflicted by the Indians to return to mental suffering inflicted by their neighbors. Their captivity over, their ordeal was just beginning.

3

AN ELITE EMERGES

I do not feel as helpless as I thought I should—when people are obliged to depend altogether upon themselves, they frequently find, that they possess resources of which they were ignorant—

Margaretta Brown, 1802

IN A REMARKABLY short time—ten to twenty years—the Kentucky frontier vanished. Forts and settlements with their scattering of log cabins were gone, replaced by busy towns with handsome brick houses. Gone, too, were frontier simplicity and egalitarianism. At the upper levels of a newly stratified society, the role of women was changing. The competence and resourcefulness of the frontier woman were no longer highly valued; women were now to be useless and decorative, living evidence of family financial success.

A wealthy and powerful class established itself in the new state. Their work done by slaves, they built large comfortable houses, importing carpets, wallpaper, curtains, pianos from the East. They educated their sons at Transylvania University, or exported them to universities back across the mountains. For their daughters, they had other plans.

According to Richard C. Wade, by 1820,

The most sheltered group in transmontane cities were the daughters of the rich, whom Mrs. Trollope called a "privileged class." Carefully guarded by socially sensitive mothers, screened from the world outside from birth, and educated in fashionable schools, they lived well removed from the rest of urban society. Leisure and frivolity increasingly occupied their time. . . . Nor did this relaxed life end with marriage. Matrimony merely set off new social rounds.

In Lexington, where Mary Austin Holley reluctantly moved when her husband became president of Transylvania in 1818, she was astonished that local ladies made morning calls in silks and satins. By Boston standards, they overdressed. Like her uncle Moses Austin a critical newcomer to Kentucky, Mrs. Holley clearly regarded her new acquaintances as pretentious, dull, perhaps a bit nouveau riche.

Nor did she care for another new feminine style: reticence and submissiveness. In the 1820s, Mrs. Holley observed without pleasure that her married daughter had accepted this growing fashion for women. A vivid personality, Mrs. Holley found the new reticence boring. Her biographer, Rebecca Smith Lee, tells us that Mrs. Holley "preferred the more forthright manners of the early Republic in which she had been reared."

Socially and culturally, among the new cities west of the Alleghenies, Lexington took the lead. Its new aristocracy was soon well known for its "charm, hospitality, and 'conscious superiority.' " As Louisville, too, became an urban center, its reputation was largely mercantile, the river bringing in trade as well as a rough-and-ready element. But Lexington called itself "the Athens of the West." Its chief intellectual distinction was Transylvania University; by the early 1820s its reputation was unrivalled west of the mountains. Its doors were closed to women, however, for many generations to come.

Young men at Transylvania could pursue law or medicine, or if they enrolled in the academic department, they could study Greek, Latin, English grammar, French, astronomy, chemistry, philosophy, general law, political economy, and many other subjects, including the Constitution of the United States. The well-stocked library offered books by the most advanced thinkers: Paine, Voltaire, Rousseau, Condorcet, Priestley, Godwin, Mary Wollstonecraft, among many others.

In contrast, Mrs. Holley's daughter and other fashionable young Lexington women were enrolled at Professor Dunham's Female Academy, where they studied history, geography, rhetoric, arithmetic, piano, drawing, and dancing—the last three regarded as "accomplishments," intended to enhance their marriageability.

For many, the round of cotillions, balls, and assemblies were all-important. Lexington's wealthy went away in the summer to resorts like Olympian Springs, in Bath County, or as far away as White Sulphur. They entertained mostly at home. Even Mrs. Holley was impressed by the country estate of Colonel David Meade, whose grounds boasted a large lake, an English hunting lodge, and Chinese and Grecian temples in the gardens. Indoors, the walls were lined with family portraits, one by Sir Joshua Reynolds. Rebecca Smith Lee describes the scene:

Mrs. Meade, in cap and ruffles, greeted them graciously, and played the pianoforte cheerfully until Old Dean, the lordly black butler, announced dinner. They sat down at four o'clock in the walnut-panelled dining room to a long table loaded with the delicacies of the region—ham and chickens, puddings and hot breads, cakes and pies. The conversation was as good as the viands.

But a distinction must be made among wives and daughters of the wealthy. Daughters might devote themselves to social rounds, with marriage—advantageous marriage—as their goal, and wives of prosperous merchants might lead a pampered life. Wives of large landholders, however, had heavy responsibilities. They might work harder than their husbands, although this fact they self-effacingly concealed. While many landholders devoted themselves to gambling, hunting, and sometimes the pursuit of women, their wives saw to it that the farms produced and that the slave work force was healthy and cared for.

One such hard-working woman was Lucretia Hart Clay.

While Henry Clay advanced his career in Washington, she spent most of the time in Lexington, running "Ashland." A hemp and stock plantation, "Ashland" made use of fifty to sixty slaves, the responsibility of Lucretia Clay.

Graced by a free and easy attitude toward money, Clay signed notes for friends rather casually. He also gambled for high stakes, once losing eight thousand dollars—a formidable amount in those days—and winning it back in one evening's play. Money did not worry him: that was Mrs. Clay's problem, and she managed the plantation with skill and frugality. Mother of eleven children, she found time to sell—often in person—butter, eggs, chickens, and vegetables to the Phoenix Hotel and other Lexington hostelries. Clay appreciated her industry, which was good political capital as well, and said of her: "Again and again she saved our home from bankruptcy."

An example of Lucretia Clay's sensible, unruffled temperament is cited by Clement Eaton: "A New England lady said to her, 'Isn't it a pity that your husband gambles so much!' 'Oh, I don't know,' she quickly replied, 'He usually wins.' "

Power and comfort did not immunize the Clays from grief. All six of their daughters died early, most as infants or girls, the last at age twenty-eight. Of their sons, one spent years in an insane asylum in Lexington, one was briefly in prison, and the most promising was killed in the Mexican War. In spite of these losses, Lucretia Clay was not embittered. Her contemporaries spoke of her as a kind woman, as well as a practical and energetic one. Without question a Kentucky aristocrat, she had no more leisure than any hardworking woman in the backwoods.

Many such backwoods women still lived primitive lives in Kentucky, untouched by the wealth and comfort of the new class of city-dwellers. A former backwoodsman who observed the swift changes in society was Daniel Drake, a distinguished physician whose first home in Kentucky was a covered sheep pen. In 1788, when his almost penniless family migrated by flatboat and wagon to Mayslick, he was three years old. People were still afraid of Indians: "The children were told at night, 'lie still and go to sleep, or the Shawnees will catch you.' " At fifteen, in 1800, he left for Cincinnati to learn to be a doctor. In that brief span of years, the frontier had disappeared. As he approached old age, Dr. Drake wrote letters to his children to record his memories of his simple pioneer boyhood and a vanished way of life.

The Drakes were producers, making everything they used. From the sheep pen, they moved to a one-room log cabin that they built themselves. Because his hard-working mother, Elizabeth, had six small children and no household help, young Daniel learned to do what was considered woman's work. As soon as his sister Lizy was old enough, these chores were handed on to her. Daniel preferred working in the fields, but he realized that his mother needed him:

I have already spoken of grating and pounding corn, toting water from a distant spring, going to the pond on wash days . . . and divers other labours with which mother was intimately connected. But my domestic occupations were far more extensive than these. To chop, split and bring in wood; keep up the fire, pick up chips in the corn basket for kindlings in the morning, and for light, through the long winter evenings when "taller" was too scarce to afford sufficient candles, and "fat" so necessary for cooking, that the boat-lamp, stuck into one of the logs of the cabin over the hearth, could not always be supplied, were regular labours. . . . To slop the cows, and when wild, drive them into a corner of the fence, and stand over them with a stick while mother milked them, was another. Occasionally I assisted her in milking, but sister Liz was taught that accomplishment as early as possible, seeing that it was held by the whole neighborhood to be quite too "gaalish" for a boy to milk; and mother, quite as much as myself, would have been mortified, if any neighbouring boy or man had caught me at it.

Daniel Drake recalled catching rainwater in tubs for washdays, hanging the wet clothes on the rail fence because they had no line, and in cold weather, bringing in the clothes, stiff and frozen. He remembered, too, hunting for hens' eggs and for greens or "sauce"—turnip greens and dandelion—for meals, cleaning the iron candlestick, tending the baby, and sweeping the floor. Since they had no clock, they decided by the shadow on the doorsill "whether it was time I should put the potatoes in." Keeping the fire going was important, for all the cooking was done at the cabin hearth:

In the morning, a buckeye backlog and hickory forestick resting on stone andirons, and with a Jonny cake on a clean ash board, set before it to bake, a frying pan with its long handle resting on a split botomed turner's chair . . . the tea kettle swung from a wooden "lug pole" with myself setting the table, or turning the meat, or watching the Jonny cake, while she [his mother] sat nursing the baby in the corner, and telling the little ones to "hold still" and let their sister Lizy dress them!

In 1788 the Drakes had been among the first to settle at Mayslick. But within six years, immigration was "immense," and "one would not wander a mile in any direction, without meeting with a clearing . . . and . . . a one story unhewed log cabin, with the latch string always out." Usually a group of "ragged children" were playing outside, for women settlers were prolific.

The Drake family enjoyed watching wagons loaded with merchandise, and travelers on horseback going through Mayslick. When they moved farther away to find more farmland, the loneliness was oppressive, especially to the mother, Elizabeth Drake: "For the first years, she felt the solitude in which we were entombed, more severely than any other member of the family. She could not go much from home, like father whom business would frequently call away, nor like myself, who was the errant boy."

One of Daniel Drake's happiest recollections was of his pioneer family bound for church:

It was a day of rest from the labours of the field. . . . It was, also, a day for dressing up, and none but those who labour through the week, in coarse and dirty clothes, can estimate the cheering influence of a clean face and feet, a clean shirt, and "boughten" clothes on a sabbath morning. . . . At length . . . we take our departure—mother in a calico dress, with her black silk bonnet covering a newly ironed cap, with the tabs (flaps) tied beneath her chin with a piece of narrow ribbon; father with his shoes just creased and blacked (by myself) with fat & soot, well mixed together; in his shirt sleeves, if the weather were hot, or in his sunday coat, if cool; roram dress-hat over his short, smooth black hair; a bandana handkerchief in his *pocket* for *that* day; and his "walking" stick in his hand, or the baby in his arms; myself in my fustian jacket; with my hat brushed and *set up*, my feet clean, and a new rag on some luckless "stubbed & festering toe"; the younger children in their best sunday clothes; and the whole of us slowly, yet cheerfully—playfully—moving onward through the cool and quiet woods to the house of God.

Although his parents were uneducated, they valued education, viewing it as a means of rising in the world. Poor as they were, and expensive as books were, the Drakes had several in their cabin. With their neighbors—"all poor and all illiterate"—they managed to start a school in a log schoolhouse. Girls as well as boys attended this country school. Bringing their "dinner," they ate outdoors in the woods in warm weather:

The meal over, then came the play & romps, in many of which the boys and girls mingled together; but sometimes the rudeness of the former drove the latter for one "dinner spell" by themselves. Swinging by grape vines was, in general, a joint amusement, as was hunting nuts, haws, paw-paws, & other fruits when in season.

One assumes that his sister Lizy was also a student, although he never mentions her. It is clear that to his family, it was Daniel's education that mattered, for his parents were determined that he should be a doctor. When Daniel was fifteen, his father took him to Cincinnati to study for that purpose.

In 1848, thinking back over his experience with coeducation in the log-cabin school, Daniel Drake's views were remarkably advanced:

It is true that the union of boys and girls within and without a country school house is not free from objections, but it is natural; and if the latter hear some things which they should not, and form some habits not befitting their sex, they become better prepared for the rough and tumble of life, in which the most favoured may be involved. Their constitutions are hardened; & their knowledge of the character of the other sex increased; while the feelings and manners of the boys are to some extent refined by the association.

Undoubtedly, Daniel Drake remembered the quiet responsibility of his mother—more responsible than his father when the going was hard—and other competent women of his frontier boyhood. In later years he became acquainted with the views of women whose ideas were advanced, even radical. Harriet Martineau visited him personally. And he had read Mary Wollstonecraft, for in describing the tedious drudgery of grinding corn, he wrote: "Mary Wolstoncraft remarks of girls that were compelled to sew a great deal, in her day, as a part of their education, that their ideas at length came to follow their needles. In like manner mine went up and down with the pestle." But in 1848, the Victorian era was well under way. Women were popularly regarded with pious sentimentality. When Dr. Drake advocated hardening the constitutions of girls and preparing them "for the rough and tumble of life, in which the most favoured may be involved," few would have agreed with him.

As his parents had dreamed, Daniel Drake rose in the world. His sister Lizy, for whom they had no dreams, did not. As a prominent physician, he was associated with the new aristocracy.

Among Drake's colleagues on the medical faculty of Transylvania University was Dr. Samuel Brown, who had given smallpox vaccinations to some five hundred Kentucky residents before doctors in the East had started vaccinating their patients. Unlike Drake's family, Brown's was a distinguished one. One brother, James, then a law professor at Transylvania, would become a United States senator from Louisiana and Monroe's minister to France. Another, John Brown, was the first United States senator from Kentucky. A well-educated lawyer from Virginia and a friend of Jefferson and Madison, John Brown had migrated to Kentucky in 1783, five years before the Drakes did so.

Senator John Brown brought his bride, Margaretta Mason Brown, to Kentucky by flatboat in 1801, a year after Dr. Drake's chronicle ends. The Drakes had lived in a sheep pen and worried about Indians, but Margaretta Brown would live in a handsome house, "Liberty Hall," still a landmark in Frankfort. She left a number of letters that depict her daily life—a life of luxury and privilege compared to that of the humble Drakes.

Leaving behind the lively society of New York City, Margaretta Brown adjusted to the village of Frankfort, soon to be a small town. While her husband spent much of his time in Washington, she had many decisions to make on her own. Her letters tell of buying hogs, having a fence built, collecting on a note, and learning, to her annoyance, that the bacon she had bought would cost fifteen shillings "and I could have purchased abundance for twelve." Before long, she acquired a sense of competence, as she wrote her husband:

I do not feel as *helpless* as I thought I should—when people are obliged to depend altogether upon themselves, they frequently find, that they possess resources of which they were ignorant— Make yourself then, my Love, as happy as possible—Unavoidable accidents excepted, I hope to make out tolerably well.

A miniature by the artist Edward West portrays Margaretta Brown as an attractive and serious woman. And serious she was. Revivalism would soon catch fire in Kentucky, but such emotional binges were not for the aristocratic Browns. Mrs. Brown's father, brother, and father-in-law were all well-educated Presbyterian ministers, and religion—a severe Presbyterian religion—was her principal interest. Indeed, she complained to her husband about the growing liberalism in New York churches. Her religion was the stern eighteenth-century variety in which she had been brought up, rather than the more liberal, sentimentalized version of the nineteenth century. It was this religion that she in turn taught Frankfort girls in the Sunday school (the first in the state) that claimed most of her energies.

For these girls—106 of them by 1832—she wrote and had printed a small book called *Food for Lambs, or Familiar Explanations of Some Religious Terms Compiled by One of Their Teachers.* To have used her own name would have been an unladylike self-assertion.

In her little book, Margaretta Brown defined such terms as "DEPRAVITY OF HUMAN NATURE: our original sin." Another familiar explanation for the young girls of Frankfort: "WORM THAT NEVER DIES: conscience. The conscience of a sinner in hell, is compared to a worm, continually gnawing his vitals; because it will forever upbraid him, with the opportunities which he has neglected."

She was delighted when one particularly pious young woman, her future daughter-in-law, memorized no fewer than 2,387 Bible and hymn verses in ten months, "besides attending other schools and getting tasks every day in the week."

Curiously, Mrs. Brown was both religious and worldly. Distinguished guests obviously pleased her, and she wrote her son Orlando in 1819 that the president of the United States, James Monroe, "breakfasted with *us*, in company with Gen[l] Jackson, and that *Hero* . . . Major Z. Taylor."

When Lafayette visited Kentucky in 1825, Margaretta Brown declined to go to a ball in his honor because of her strict Presbyterian views about dancing. She wrote her stepmother in New York, "they all paraded [to] the Ball . . . when who should arrive here but General Lafayette, his son and suite. The General spent nearly an hour with us in most delightful conversation, while those who went to the Ball did not exchange a sylable with him. Had I not a triumph?"

40

In principle egalitarian, she found that in practice, democracy was not so pleasant. Of an assembly in Frankfort in 1802, she wrote her husband:

It was tolerably agreeable. We had twenty-two ladies, and as many gentlemen . . . Mr Blair was my escort . . . Mr *Pearson* (the *tavern keeper*) was there also. He is probably looking out for another wife. This *equality*, my Love, is a mighty *pretty* thing upon *paper*, and a very useful thing in the common intercourses of life, but does not suit a regular Assembly quite so well. But I will say no more upon this subject; fortunately recollecting, that you once gave me a serious lecture, for some of my Aristocratic notions.

In time, however, she would accept no criticism of her adopted state. Writing a niece in New York in 1832, she scoffed at Mrs. Trollope's recently published views of the West—but she admitted one reservation: "In one thing however I agree with her—No disgust can be too great nor any language too indignant to express the loathing which I have against *tobacco spitting.*"

Margaretta Brown's worldliness is evident in her assumption that the business of young women was to marry, and furthermore, to marry suitably and well. To her New York niece she wrote: "From a story in one of the N.Y. papers I learned that one of her [a cousin's] daughters was married. I have never heard whether the connexion she formed was advantageous, and shall be glad to be informed on the subject." And writing her husband that a young friend was to be married, she told him: "I think she may do better by waiting." In another report to New York, she told of two young Frankfort women who stayed away from the dances held during the legislative session and whose piety led to worldly success:

Miss Harvie (the least attractive of our young ladies in point of personal charms, though a religious and amiable girl) married very well, during the sitting of the Legislature. . . . Another young Lady who spent the winter with her, is also married to Mr Trotter, a young Presbyterian Clergyman—These young Ladies were both professors of religion; and did not engage in any of the dissipations of the Season—and they are the only two, who have acquired what most gay young Ladies are in pursuit of—a good establishment.

Protected by comfort and security beyond the dreams of most women of her time, and spared the burden of heavy physical work that was the lot of many, Margaretta Brown was as vulnerable as any other woman to the death of children. Disease made young lives precarious. Even the sturdiest might die suddenly.

The Browns had the best medical care of the day. Although medicine was still primitive, it was making some advances, as Dr. Samuel Brown's work with smallpox vaccination indicates. Surgery, too, was rudimentary, although at Danville in 1809, Dr. Ephraim McDowell had performed a remarkable operation: the first ovariotomy. Without anesthesia, he removed a twenty-two-pound tumor from Jane Todd Crawford of Green County, a hardy farm woman who outlived the surgeon by ten years.

But most diseases were still a mystery. In the summer of 1833, when a terrible epidemic of cholera killed hundreds in Kentucky, Mrs. Brown wrote her niece in New York: "That dreadful scourge is raging in an awful manner—amongst us." She mentions, in her letters, other diseases from time to time: whooping cough, measles, scarlet fever, ague. Dr. Brown's own wife died of some illness in pregnancy, and Judith, wife of Margaretta Brown's elder son, Mason, died young of tuberculosis. After Judith's death, the rearing of Mason's small son, Gratz Brown, fell to his grandmother.

Serious Presbyterian that she was, Mrs. Brown had a gentle sense of humor that could be evoked by this grandson. Away on a trip, she sent him an affectionate message in a letter to the family:

I am told too, that [at White Sulphur] you have to encounter hordes of vermin, which is a most appalling circumstance to me— Hitherto I have been so fortunate as not to be annoyed by a single insect in all our journey—Tell Gratz that I have not seen a single flea since I left home, the consequence, I suppose, of having met with no house dogs—nor kept company with any little folks [i.e. her grandson] who frequented the stable lot.

Once the lively Gratz, his grandmother wrote, "fell from an Apple tree, upwards of Twenty feet—broke his right thigh, and received a wound of more than an inch in length, under his chin, which penetrated to his tongue." He recovered slowly, his grandmother devotedly caring for him during his convalescence.

Her dedication to this grandchild was doubtless increased by the deaths, in the past, among her own children. After two sons died, at ages eleven months and two months, Margaretta Brown expressed, in the last poem of a small book of her verses, the fears she held for her newborn daughter, Euphemia. But Euphemia survived the risks of infancy, growing into a bright and promising child and a great favorite. Her sudden illness and death at age seven—partly caused by an overdose of calomel—had a lasting effect on her parents. Four years afterward, Mrs. Brown's brother wrote of this death: "Her [Margaretta's] vivacity has greatly subsided. . . . Mr. B. himself even to this hour, is almost unmanned by it."

The Browns, in vigorous health, made long journeys back East even when they were quite old. In an era when travel conditions were arduous, they traveled tirelessly. And when they traveled, they bought—for themselves, for their relatives, for their home.

Whereas Daniel Drake's family were producers, making everything they used, the Brown family were consumers, and in large volume. In 1836, at ages sixty-four and seventy-nine, Margaretta and John Brown took a trip to New York, buying a piano for $300 for one daughter-in-law, and $500 worth of silver for the other. They also bought two bales of carpeting, a pair of mirrors for $160, sixty pieces of wallpaper, books, a globe for Gratz.

Just a year before, John Brown had returned from the

East "loaded with presents for us all," as a nephew wrote home:

In the first place dear Ma just think of an *elegant* gold watch and seals—(He brought Aunt one also)—5 dozen silver spoons small & large ladle &c Silver (plated Coffee, tea pots, sugar dish sug tongs &c—a complete set of dinner china & tea sets (Newest style nest of beautiful waiters, casters, silver fruit baskets 4 vases—4 candlesticks, and many other, little things besides two pieces of fine linen—a piece of sheeting 6 pair of silk stockings &c. . . . I cant tell you all that Aunt got—but I thought of you when the beautiful caps were exhibited—she has the most splendid carpet that I ever saw for her drawing room.

This astonishing height of consumerism was reached only a few years after Daniel Drake's mother had baked "Jonny cake on a clean ash board" and stirred meal in an iron mush pot at the hearth, while the family ate with "the dull clatter of pewter spoons in pewter basins."

The frontier lay far behind. Margaretta Brown was a woman of the immediate future. She would not have agreed with Dr. Drake's views on preparing girls "for the rough and tumble of life, in which the most favoured may be involved." Well aware, however, of her own intelligence, she once reported of a "very brilliant party" in New York:

I was introduced to Mr *Sampson*, his wife, and daughter, and conversed a good deal with them. He does not appear to great advantage in conversation—I heard him make no remarks, but what were quite common-place (but perhaps he recollected that he was talking to a *woman*).

Nevertheless, she accepted the concept that a woman's sphere was in the home, as a consumer and as an influence—a pious influence.

And probably her influence helped shape the character of her much loved grandson, Gratz. Educated at Transylvania and at Yale, he became governor of Missouri, and like his

Kentucky grandfather, United States senator. On the question of slavery, he worked his way from a belief in gradual emancipation to an abolitionist position. In the United States Senate in 1867, he spoke in favor of suffrage rights for all, not only for white and black males, but even for women: "I am willing to express an opinion very freely on this subject. . . . I stand for Universal Suffrage, and as a matter of fundamental principle do not recognize the right of society to limit it on any grounds of race, color or sex." His biographer tells us that he refuted the objection that women should not vote because they do not bear arms by simply pointing to all the Senators who had not fought in a war and noting that they were nevertheless serving in the Senate.

More than half a century would pass before society would accept Gratz Brown's vision. It is likely that he arrived at it so early because his boyhood years with his intelligent and high-principled grandmother taught him that a woman can be anyone's equal.

Although Margaretta Brown combined the qualities of piety and worldliness, not everyone could resolve these conflicting claims. Turning their backs on the increasing complexity and materialism of society, some Kentucky women chose instead simplicity, austerity, and a sense of purpose. For such a life, they abandoned the world for communal living with others who shared their values. Some were Catholics; some were Shakers.

After several early efforts by missionary priests to establish a Catholic convent in Kentucky, two orders founded convents within a year, in 1812. The first was the Sisterhood of Loretto in Marion County, a teaching order that soon branched out into a number of colonies. Next was the Sisters of Charity of Nazareth, near Bardstown. Besides establishing teaching academies and orphanages, members of the Nazareth order served as nurses in the cholera epidemic of 1833 and among the wounded in Kentucky's Civil War battles. Founded by priests who were their ecclesiastical superiors, these early convents were joined in large part by daughters of Maryland immigrants who had settled in Nelson and Marion counties and the surrounding area.

In Kentucky's two Shaker communities, South Union in Logan County and Pleasant Hill in Mercer County, women led strictly ordered, yet egalitarian, lives. Taking root in the state in the wake of the revivalism in the early years of the century, the hardworking, celibate Shakers established a dual order. Eldresses and elders directed them, and women and men had "perfect equality of rights."

Originally led by Mother Ann Lee, Shakers maintained convictions of a dual deity and dual messiahship, in the "joint parentage" of Jesus and Mother Ann, and a quaternity of Father, Son, Holy Mother Wisdom, and Daughter. In the quietude of their prosperous villages, Shaker women held a status unmatched in the outside world.

At the opposite of these productive, dedicated lives was the life of the antebellum southern belle. Sallie Ward was an archetype of this species. Born in 1827 near Georgetown, she was brought up in her father's Louisville mansion at Second and Walnut. The huge home, containing aviaries and conservatories, was the site of lavish entertaining. Educated at a French finishing school, Sallie Ward traveled with her family, accompanied by many servants, to White Sulphur in the summers and to New Orleans at Mardi Gras season.

To the delight of scandal-mongers, she married four times, applying successfully to the Kentucky legislature for a divorce from her first husband. He was a proper Bostonian, and Boston did not appreciate her. Deliberately she shocked the social world there, once appearing at a ball in an outfit recently invented by Mrs. Amelia Bloomer. And if bloomers were not enough, Bostonians whispered that she "painted." (She did.)

But back in Kentucky, Sallie Ward was adored. Anything superlative was called a "Sallie Ward": livestock, steamboats, racehorses, and children were named for her. There was a Sallie Ward slipper, a Sallie Ward walk, a Sallie Ward lavender.

Given to pranks and feats of horsemanship, she had a shrewd sense of stagecraft. After her divorce, she retired from society for a time. She reappeared at a Louisville ball, delaying her entrance until after midnight. Then, as the music stopped, silence fell on the ballroom, and the whisper "Sallie Ward" went up, she descended the stairs in a magnificent dress of virginal white tulle, on the arm of an attractive man.

And on another occasion, a fancy dress ball in Lexington, she changed costume four times during the evening, capping her performance by appearing as a houri.

Sallie Ward next married a rich physician in New Orleans, and she dazzled even that jaded city with social coups of daring magnitude: she was the first to use opera glasses in New Orleans, and the first to have an orchestra play during lavish dinner parties. Widowed twice, she married a fourth time and spent the rest of her long life in Louisville, the charming, spoiled darling of the community until the end.

The belle flourished in an elite world of sentimental adulation of female purity and male code of honor—concepts romantic enough in the abstract, but in practice, effective means of controlling women. Her uselessness and ornamentality served as proof of her family's affluence and position. But as other, imitation Sallie Wards would find, the Civil War blighted the belle industry.

4

SLAVE STATE

*She was handcuffed and got away at Ruddles Mills on her
way down the river, which is the fifth time she escaped
when about to be sent out of the country.*
Advertisement for Sarah, 1822

IN THE KENTUCKY social hierarchy, most powerless were
black women. Subject to all of the abuses of slavery, they
were vulnerable to additional ones as women. It was widely
known, for example, that the slave trader Lewis Robards of
Lexington sold black women into prostitution—a practice
in which no one intervened—and other traders operated
breeding farms for southern markets. Moreover, the exploitation of black women by their owners was not unusual, as
evidenced by numbers of nearly white slave children. In a
world in which black women were degraded in many ways,
theirs was a difficult struggle to preserve family ties and
self-esteem.

Uneasy knowledge of owners' exploitation of black wom-
en ran through communities, and slaves themselves often
knew the identity of their white fathers. The former slave
William Wells Brown wrote of his birth in Lexington:

My mother's name was Elizabeth. . . . She had seven children. . . . No two of us were children of the same father. My father's name, as I learned from my mother, was George Higgins. He
was a white man, a relative of my master, and connected with
some of the first families in Kentucky.

Of her paternity, another former slave, Nannie Eaves of Hopkinsville, recalled in the slave narratives recorded in the 1930s:

I was never once treated as a slave because my master was my very own daddy. Ben Eaves, my husband, was a slave and child of George Eaves, my master's brother. He ran away from his master and his daddy and joined the U.S. Army during the Secess War.

These narratives, often recorded in an inconsistent attempt at dialect, have been criticized because the former slaves may have tried to give the interviewers what they seemed to want to hear: that slavery was a benign institution. But accounts of former slave women in Kentucky were seldom favorable. Nannie Eaves claimed special protection because of her paternity. But other slave children of white owners were less fortunate.

Public auction blocks in Kentucky towns served as reminders of the institution to which the state was bound—distressing reminders, especially when the auction victims were almost white. The sales in Lexington of Eliza, only one sixty-fourth black, and of two sisters who were graduates of Oberlin College—all three the daughters of their white masters—were causes célèbres, as J. Winston Coleman, Jr., relates in *Slavery Times in Kentucky*. But black women, children, and men were sold every court-day, and no one turned a head. It was whiteness, the obvious kinship with the white ruling class, that distressed onlookers.

Although evidence of such kinship stood often enough on the auction block, the dread of miscegenation nevertheless took on the obsessive proportions of a powerful myth. Boynton Merrill, Jr., in *Jefferson's Nephews: A Frontier Tragedy*, a work that deals with slavery in Kentucky, writes that this dread is grounded in "the fear that the two races, given the chance, would blend and supposedly corrupt the genetic reservoir of the white race." The author maintains that the fear of miscegenation has "its roots deep in the conviction of white superiority." He acknowledges the inconsistency here, given the fact that the taboo applied only to white women and black men, and not to white men and black women. But it seems obvious that this inconsistency makes the theory meaningless.

The taboo against miscegenation had nothing to do with the mixing of races. That mixing had gone on from the beginning, from the time the first white owner made his way to the slave quarters after dark.

The roots of the fear of miscegenation clearly lay elsewhere: in the control of women. Partly it originated in the belief that women are property. Partly, too, as with white attitudes toward Indians in the previous century, perhaps the black man was viewed as closer to nature and the possessor of a primitive power that threatened white males. The obsession took on excessive emotional proportions because it was based not "deep in the conviction of white superiority" but deep in doubts about it.

That uneasy superiority was enforced by the threat of sale. A former slave, Amelia Jones of Laurel County, recalled that her owner

didn't hesitate to sell any of his slaves. He said, "You all belong to me and if you don't like it, I'll put you in my pocket," meaning of course that he would sell that slave and put the money in his pocket. The day he was to sell the children from their mother he would tell that mother to go to some other place to do some work and in her absence he would sell the children. It was the same when he would sell a man's wife, he also sent him to another job and when he returned his wife would be gone. The master would only say, "Don't worry you can get another one."

Mrs. Jones's father was sold at auction in Manchester, handcuffed, and marched South. She never saw him again.

Another ex-slave, Mary Wooldridge, born in Washington County, related how she and her twin sister were sold in Lexington when they were fourteen. They, too, never saw each other again.

In spite of their vulnerability, some slave women resisted, covertly or overtly, and struggled for self-esteem. Sophia Ward, born in Clay County in 1837, remembered:

One day my Mistress Lyndia called for me to come in the house, but no, I wouldn't go. She walks out and says she is going make me go. So she takes and drags me in the house. Then I grab that white woman, when she turned her back, and shook her until she begged for mercy. When the master comes in, I was given a terrible beating with a whip but I didn't care, for I gave the mistress a good one too.

In small ways as well, Sophia Ward resisted her role: "We would slip in the house after the master and mistress was sleeping and cook to suit ourselves and cook what we wanted." As a young girl, she took a quiet revenge for a beating:

The mistress had an old parrot and one day I was in the kitchen making cookies, and I decided I wanted some of them, so I took out some and put them on a chair; and when I did this the mistress entered the door. I pick up a cushion and throw over the pile of cookies on the chair, and Mistress came near the chair and the old parrot cries out, "Mistress burn, Mistress burn." Then the mistress looks under the cushion, and she had me whipped, but the next day I killed the parrot, and she often wondered who or what killed the bird.

With pride, Sophia Ward claimed that "the white folks said I was the meanest nigger that ever was."

Rebellion of monumental proportions was created by Sarah, a Bourbon County woman who resisted slavery with ferocity. In an advertisement offering a $50 reward for her capture in 1822, her owner said that she was about six feet tall, "very slim," with "white eyes":

Sarah is the biggest devil that ever lived, having poisoned a stud horse and set a stable on fire, also burnt Gen. R. Williams stable and stack yard with seven horses and other property to value of

$1500. She was handcuffed and got away at Ruddles Mills on her way down the river, which is the fifth time she escaped when about to be sent out of the country.

Although not openly rebellious, another former slave, Annie B. Boyd of Hopkinsville, remembered her mistress with anger:

The white folks weren't good to me. My master was a good man but my mistress wasn't a good woman. She used to box my ears, stick pins in me and tie me to the cedar chest and whip me as long as she wanted. Oh, how I did hate that woman.

Once when Annie B. Boyd was supposed to be watching a baby, the child bit into an Indian turnip. Her mistress forced Annie Boyd to eat the rest of the turnip, causing the slave's face to swell painfully. She had angry memories of the evenings also:

After nursing the baby and tending to the other children all the day, at night when I put the baby to bed I had to knit two rounds every night and would be sleepy and my mistress would reach over and jab a pin in me to keep me awake. Now that is what I call a mean woman.

A former slave who was born in Burkesville and sold to Missouri, Jane Simpson said of her mistress: "If Old Miss got mad about something, just anything at all, she'd have you whipped, when maybe you had not done a thing, just to satisfy her spite feeling."

Other slaves recalled happier relationships. One was Harriet Mason of Garrard County:

My master was a preacher and a doctor and a fine man. Miss Mat was hard to beat. . . . My mistress taught all the slaves to read and write, and we sat on a bench in the dining room. . . .

At Christmas and New Years we did have big times, and General Gano and Miss Mat would buy us candy, popcorn, and firecrackers and all the good things just like the white folks.

52

Her owners never whipped a slave, Mrs. Mason said, and punishments were mild:

One time I was acting nurse for Mistress, there was another nigger girl there and we was playing horse-shoes. Celia hit me in the head. It got blood all over the baby's dress. Miss came out, she says, "I'll hit you niggers if you don't stop playing with horseshoes." The scar is on my head yet where Celia hit me. I ain't played since.

Missis told her brother Sam one day to whip me. Every time he hit me, I'd hit him. I wasn't feared then. I didn't know any better.

Ann Gudgel of Anderson County was beaten once, but she seemed to think she deserved punishment:

Mammy worked up at the big house, but we children had to stay at the cabin. But I didn't very much care, because ole Miss had a little child just about my age, and we played together. The only time ole Miss ever beat me was when I caused Miss Nancy to get eaten up with the bees. I told her, "Miss Nancy, the bees are asleep, let's steal the honey." Soon as she touched it, they flew all over us, and it took Mammy about a day to get the stingers out of our heads. Ole Miss just naturally beat me up about that.

Although some slaves reported that they had never seen a whipping, others saw many. Joana Owens of Hawesville remembered that when her owner, Nolan Barr, "got mad at his slaves for not working hard enough he would tie them up by their thumbs and whip the male slaves till they begged for mercy." Edd Shirley of Tompkinsville recalled that "I once saw a light colored girl tied to the rafters of a barn, and her master whipped her until blood ran down her back and made a large pool on the ground." And Sophia Ward said:

My master wasn't as mean as most masters. Hugh White was so mean to his slaves that I know of two girls that killed themselves. One nigger girl Sudie was found across the bed with a pen knife in her hand. He whipped another nigger girl almost to death, for forgetting to put onions in the stew. The next day she went down to the river and for nine days they searched for her and her body finally washed up on the shore.

White felt haunted by this woman, according to Sophia Ward, and later hanged himself.

However, the sadistic owner was unusual. Most slaves were valuable property. At the Civil War, 225,483 slaves lived in the state, owned by 38,645 Kentuckians—more slaveholders than in any other state except Virginia and Georgia, as Steven A. Channing has observed. Although large plantations were impractical in Kentucky, ownership of small groups of slaves made farms profitable.

Although women might work in the fields, most farm work was done by men. Belle Robinson of Garrard County gave a typical account of this division of labor: "My mother and father lived at the cabin in the yard and my mother did the cooking for the family. My father did the work on the farm with the help that was hired from the neighbors."

As a small child, Jane Simpson did some outdoor work:

I wasn't old enough to be much help, till I became the property of Marse Cook. Then I was big enough to pick up chunks in the field, set brush heaps afire, burn up rubbish, pull weeds, and the like. He sold me to Dr. Hart around the age of ten to be his house girl.

Susan Dale Sanders of Taylorsville considered field work for women a cruel rarity: "Some of the other old Masters, who had lots of slaves on farms close by, were so mean to the slaves they owned. They worked the women and men both in the fields and the children too." Joana Owens of Hawesville also thought such work cruel: "I will never forget how mean old Master Nolan Barr was to us. My mother did the housework. . . . My father and sister and I had to work in the fields." But field chores were commonplace to Mary Wooldridge when she worked on Thomas McElroy's large farm near Lexington: "My master has his nigger girls to lay fence worms, make fences, shuck corn, hoe corn and tobacco, wash, iron, and the mistress tried to teach the nigger girls to sew and knit."

Because Kentucky farms were not large plantations, household service seems more usual for Kentucky slave women. Susan Dale Sanders's father was a field worker, but the women in her family did housework:

I used to carry tubs of clothes down to the old spring house, there was plenty of water, and I washed all the clothes there. I and my sisters used to wash and sing and we had a good time. Mammy worked hard, did all the cooking.

A house servant might draw status from her position, identify with her owners, and reject her own people. One who clearly did so was Harriet Mason, who felt superiority in her ability to read and write and in her position as nurse to the white children. "When the news came that we were free General Gano called us all in the dining room and told us about it. I told him I wasn't going to the cabins and sleep with them niggers and I didn't." Although Belle Robinson's parents lived in a cabin, she emphasized that "I was the only child and had always lived at the big house with my mistress. I wore the same kind of clothes and ate the same kind of food the white people ate." And Kate Billingsby of Hopkinsville also stressed the fact that she was "raised in the white folks house": "No I don't believe in ghosts, haunts, or anything of that kind, my white folks being 'quality.' I been raised by 'quality!' Why I'm a 'quality nigger.' " But a former field worker, Mary Wooldridge, resented the snobbishness of house servants: "All these ole niggers try to be so uppity by just being raised in the house and because they were, why they think [they] are quality."

Although house servants had higher status and supposedly better lives than field workers, slaves in other states—the articulate Lewis Clarke, for example—spoke of the stress of being constantly on duty at the owner's elbow. It was no pleasure to be around white people all of the time, subject to their moods and vagaries.

In spite of the indignities that beset slaves and the vulnerability of their families, the slave family was a significant institution. In interviews, former Kentucky slaves listed relatives, described the backgrounds of their mothers and fathers, and often mentioned that they lived with both parents. Although Kentucky law forbade slave marriages and acknowledged no ties between slave parents and children, slave marriages were socially, if not legally, recognized. Unlike other border states, Kentucky did not free its slaves during the Civil War, and it was not until December 18, 1865, that slaves were emancipated and their marriages could be registered. Herbert G. Gutman, in *The Black Family in Slavery and Freedom: 1750-1925*, notes that when Congress freed wives and children of slave soldiers in March of 1865, Kentucky slaves flocked to Union camps to be married legally.

Even when slave couples belonged to different owners, they still might maintain a home. Susan Dale Sanders kept her mother's name, Dale, because that was the name of their owner. Her father was a slave on a farm nearby:

Mammy was allowed to marry one of the Allen slaves. My father had to stay at his master's . . . and work in the fields all day, but at night he would come to my mammy's cabin and stay all night, and go back to his master's . . . fields the next morning.

Looking back, Annie B. Boyd resented such arrangements as degrading:

The white folks just made niggers carry on like brutes. One white man used to say to another white man, "My nigger man Sam wants to marry your nigger girl Lucy, what do you say" and if he said it was all right, why that couple was supposed to be married. Then Sam would work for his master in the daytime and then would spend the night at Lucy's house on the next plantation.

Other former slaves regarded these marriages as binding. Even though legally unsanctioned, ceremonies might be held. Annie Morgan of Hopkinsville was married after the war but in the old way: "When I and my man were married, all the colored folks in the neighborhood come to Ma's and we—my husband and me—jumped over the broom stick and we have been married, ever since. . . . most colored folks married that way." Born in 1828, Kate Billingsby "was married by Mr. Alexander at McClain College. I was a cook and he was the janitor. My man followed his Master in the Secess War." Mary Wright of Gracey said of her parents' wedding, "my Pappy's master ask my Mammy's master for her and then my Mammy's Master gave her a big affair that cost him $200 with the bridal supper and all." And a Mrs. Heyburn of Union County recalled that "one of the daughters of the slaves was married in the kitchen of my grandfather's house. After the wedding they set supper for them."

But all slave-master relationships were not so benign, and Kentucky owners dreaded slave uprisings. Like other slaveholders, they feared poisonings and the hand raised against an owner that might begin some frightful massacre. Coleman tells of a Lexington woman from Massachusetts, Caroline Turner, despised by whites for her insanely sadistic treatment of slaves. While she was whipping a young coachman in chains early one morning, he broke free and strangled her. Sympathetic as they had previously been toward the Turner slaves, Lexington citizens quickly closed ranks to hunt the young slave down and have him hanged.

Even though Margaretta Brown disliked slavery and favored gradual emancipation, she dreaded an uprising. In a letter to her husband she observed that "the *Monster* Slavery [may] destroy the people of Ken^y before long." And writing her niece in New York City, she complained in 1834 about a young Presbyterian minister, Mr. Davidson, who made what she considered an inflammatory abolitionist talk in church, "*all this to Galleries overflowing with Negroes*":

The cause of gradual emancipation is gaining ground daily in the West, but these premature and violent measures, will have a tendency to create such a spirit of insubordination amongst the slaves, as will render it necessary to rivet their chains more closely in order to our self preservation, or they will be stimulated to take their cause in their own hands and the tragedy of St. Domingo may indeed be reacted here.

While debates raged among white Kentuckians about solutions to slavery, some slaves acted. Crossing the state's long borders into free states were the runaways. Advertisements in newspapers indicate that about eleven percent of all runaway slaves were women. Sarah of Bourbon County was a memorable example, and there were others. In 1852, *The Voice of the Fugitive*, published in Ontario by Henry Bibb, an escaped slave from Shelby County, ran an announcement:

We are happy to announce the arrival of eight females by the last train of the Underground Railroad from Kentucky. They are all one family consisting of a mother and her daughters . . . and it has scarcely ever been our lot to witness such a respectable and intelligent family of females from slavery . . . they will be an ornament in the future to our social circle in Canada.

Some free blacks living marginally in Kentucky did what they could to relieve others in bondage by buying them from white masters. The census of 1830 revealed that among slave-owning freed slaves in Kentucky were at least eighteen women, mostly in Lexington. Usually they owned only one or two slaves, though Jane Brittain of Lexington owned four and Betty Tutt of Woodford County owned seven. Perhaps these women worked them. But the ages of these slaves owned by freed black women—ranging up to 100 in several cases—suggest otherwise. One may surmise that an aged slave, of little value to a white owner, for a small price might be rescued from slavery. An example of such motivation was Jane Slaughter's purchase, in 1850, of her own father in Lexington. Property transfer records state that she bought him from "motives of benevolence and humanity."

What was the solution to slavery? A plan to resettle slaves in Liberia stirred much interest, and by 1845, Kentucky residents had raised $5,000 to buy a tract to be called "Kentucky in Liberia." Its capital was to be named "Clay Ashland," after Henry Clay, who supported the colonization project. Himself owner of fifty to sixty slaves, Clay believed that the Liberia plan was "the only remedy for a chronic disease."

This plan caught the imagination of Emily Thomas Tubman of Frankfort, who decided to offer resettlement, as a choice, to the 164 Georgia slaves now her property as a widow. Hers was not a decision based on ideology—she later was a generous supporter of the Confederacy—but on a natural humanity. Her world had always been based on slavery: she lived in Frankfort until she was twenty-four, and then, as a young married woman, in Augusta, Georgia. She made long yearly visits to Frankfort, during which she contributed with characteristic generosity to such Kentucky institutions as Transylvania University and the new orphans' school in Midway. And in Frankfort she heard the arguments for Liberia.

By 1855, a fresh demand for slaves in the deep South had increased their value; thus 164 well-cared-for slaves represented a sizeable fortune. But Mrs. Tubman's chief concern was not whether, but how, to free her slaves. The life of a freed slave was precarious in the deep South, and Liberia seemed the answer.

Leasing a ship for about $6,000, a substantial sum for those times, Mrs. Tubman arranged for resettlement. Eighty-nine of her slaves chose to sail; the rest elected to stay with her. In 1961, 107 years after the migration, the president of Liberia came to the United States to represent his nation. He was William V. S. Tubman, descendant of two of the slaves freed by Mrs. Tubman.

Generally, however, the colonization attempt in Liberia was a failure. The expense of transportation, the increased value of slaves, and the natural reluctance of blacks themselves to settle in a strange land contributed to the demise of a project that seems fantastic in retrospect. From Kentucky, only 658 slaves had gone to Liberia when the Civil War began.

Still another approach to slavery was that of the abolitionists. A number of native Kentuckians were active in the antislavery movement over the years, and others came from outside the state. One was Delia Anne Webster, called the "petticoat abolitionist"—a term of double opprobrium.

A Vermont native, Delia Webster ran the Lexington Female Academy. In 1844, she and an abolitionist minister, Calvin Fairbank, rented horses and a buggy and pretended to elope. Just after dark they picked up Lewis Hayden, a waiter at the popular Phoenix Hotel, Harriet Hayden, and their ten-year-old son, Jo, and headed north for Ohio.

The Haydens escaped to Massachusetts, where they became active in the Underground Railroad. Fairbank was sentenced to fifteen years, Delia Webster—benefitting from the code of chivalry—to two. Although the governor said she had "desecrated" her sex, he soon pardoned her, and she returned to helping fugitive slaves, this time from a farm in Trimble County, on the Ohio River. Jailed again, she was discharged and reported "still alive and unsubdued." Once more she began to assist runaways, and eventually she herself had to escape from Kentucky, pursued by a posse. Abolition in Kentucky was a failure.

In the devastating war it took to free the slaves, many black men were impressed into or enlisted in the Union army, and black women were bystanders who often suffered. Gutman tells that after the emancipation of Kentucky slaves in 1865, some Nicholas County whites raped newly freed black women. During the war itself, black women journeyed in droves to Camp Nelson, where their husbands or sons were training as Union soldiers. The Union commander, Speed S. Fry, called this situation the "Nigger Woman Question." He expelled the women and had those who returned whipped. But the strength of family ties led more black women and children to Camp Nelson, where they settled in small huts they themselves put up near the camp. Living conditions were miserable, and most were penniless. One old woman with several sons in the Union army washed and sewed to pay her way.

Without giving these people time to collect their meager belongings, the Union commander evicted 400 of them in late November, 1864. Gutman tells that they were "dumped" from wagons on roadsides "in extreme cold weather." They suffered intensely. Having no other place to turn, about 250 made their way back to the camp. Of these, 102 died.

Still they came, often turned out by their former owners when slave husbands joined the Union army. By January, 1865, Camp Nelson was the residence of 3,060 slaves, mostly women and children.

Those who maintain that slavery in Kentucky was mild and largely benign must argue away the fact that by mid-July, 1865, 5,000 Kentucky blacks—men, women, and children—had crossed the Ohio River at Louisville. Their welcome to the North seems problematic: a *New York Times* writer referred to these people as "black vomit." Gutman notes that when travel passes were permitted blacks in Kentucky in July, 1865, many thought that these were "free papers," and roads were "literally filled" with blacks seeking permits. In Paris they created "a perfect jam" around the military office. And by November, from ten to twenty thousand Kentucky blacks had left the state for the North.

The war also brought profound changes to white women. In the North, with men in the army, women left their homes to become nurses, teachers, government office workers. In the South, where women were hedged about by rigid notions of propriety, they were far less active in the war: nursing, for example, was considered improper for young, unmarried women.

Although Kentucky stayed in the Union, it shared Southern views about ladylike behavior. Nevertheless, many Kentucky women took over the running of stores, schools, and farms when men entered Northern or Southern armies.

One woman who took an active part in the war was Margaret Breckinridge of Lexington's divided Breckinridge family. Although young and unmarried, she went South to nurse Union casualties. Although she had strong Lexington connections, her real home was in the East, and she was not restrained by Southern chivalry. In the summer and fall of 1862, she worked in hospitals in Lexington and later nursed on hospital transports bringing Union casualties up the Mississippi. Her work received much acclaim.

And many women whose role could be only that of bystander nevertheless suffered in the war. In Lexington's Gratz Park, Henrietta Morgan's handsome house was a center for Southern sympathizers. Her six Confederate sons ranged from the eldest, General John Hunt Morgan, down to Key Morgan, who enlisted at fifteen, and her two daughters were married to Confederate generals. Mrs. Morgan's home was frequently searched, and she was subjected to harassment. By the end of the war, two of her sons had been killed, and all six of her other sons and sons-in-law had been wounded. The family was to acquire fame again in a peaceful pursuit when Mrs. Morgan's grandson, Thomas Hunt Morgan, born in her house the year after the war ended, won a Nobel Prize for his research in genetics.

In all of the wartime accounts of Kentucky women of leisure, both pro-Union and pro-Confederate, one finds much flag-waving, ribbon-wearing, and singing of patriotic songs. In the bitterly divided state, women urged men to enlist, performed in "tableaux," traded insults with former friends, spied on neighbors. It all seems childish and petty. But these women had no direct way of participating in the events around them, and hatred flowed through their communities. Denied action, they turned to the mock warfare of the powerless.

Lizzie Hardin of Harrodsburg provides an interesting example of this vicarious warfare. In her journal, she tells of walking in the countryside with some women friends, and wondering what it would be like to be a soldier:

I tried to fancy how I would feel, belonging to a body of soldiers, ordered to charge up such a hill, under a heavy fire from the summit. . . . Reaching the summit, I imagined myself in the much more pleasant position of firing down on the enemy. . . . Then I tried charging down the knob, but noticing my accelerated speed, as I neared the bottom, I inwardly hoped I might not be received on fixed bayonets. After these extensive military operations, our lagging steps were turned upon the homeward march.

Conjuring up romantic visions of war ("the warlike trumpet. . . . the bloody field of victory"), Lizzie fretted about her limited role in what she saw as a thrilling conflict:

Instead of arming them [Confederate soldiers] like the Spartan women with the words "Return with thy shield or upon it," to make them calico shirts; instead of giving them our hair for bowstrings, to send them needle books and tobacco pouches. . . . And still the sewing (a woman's part in peace or war) went on.

When trainloads of Confederate soldiers passed through Harrodsburg, Lizzie Hardin and others rushed to the depot to wave their handkerchiefs. No one asked for her hair for bowstrings, but a soldier gave her a small flag, and another "promised me a pet Yankee . . . he would bring him young so I could train him up to suit myself."

Like women of leisure throughout the country, Harrodsburg women busied themselves with "relief work." Although the effects of the blockade were felt before long, luxuries were available for a time:

A new interest too we had in preparing for the sick soldiers. Relief Societies were organized throughout the South, provisions for the sick, bandages, lint, pickles, wines, jellies, clothing, everything in short which could add to their comfort was sent on in boxes. Knitting was the favorite occupation of the young ladies.

Hopes were high, and the war seemed thrilling to a young woman with many friends and relatives in the Confederate army. Lizzie Hardin followed with keen interest the career of her first cousin, Ben Hardin Helm. Married to Emilie Todd, Mary Todd Lincoln's half-sister, Helm became a Confederate general and was killed at Chickamauga. Lizzie recruited every young man she knew, even encouraging the enlistment of another cousin, sixteen-year-old Kit, who was so small that he looked twelve. Kit managed to enlist with Morgan, and before long, he, too, was killed.

Hatred divided Harrodsburg residents. Lizzie and her sister Jimmie refused to go to the Methodist Church "because the preacher was a Union man." Instead they attended Presbyterian services, at which the minister "came as near praying for the Secessionists as he dared." When the pro-Union Home Guard began arresting Confederate sympathizers, bitterness among neighbors and former friends was such that both sides "racked their brains for words in which to vent their hatred. I do not know what they said of us but if words had the power to kill Harrodsburg would have been strewn with the dead bodies of the Unionists."

But in spite of the tension—when even wife and husband might be at odds—Lizzie and Jimmie found that Harrodsburg women were still able to laugh:

In the evening while out walking we passed the house of a Secessionist and, judging from the sounds of laughter whom we would meet, we went in finding as expected a crowd of ladies comforting their despair by recounting how they had defied the Home Guard even in their hour of triumph.

Mrs. P. came in directly after us. She and all her family were Secessionists, her brothers being in our army. Her husband having drunk until he had no better sense was in the Home Guard.

"Come in," said the lady of the house to her. "Your husband has mine and has gone off to prison with him."

"Yes," said Mrs. Pulliam, "I heard one of the prisoners threatened to whip Mr. Pulliam. I wish from my heart he had done it."

At home, Lizzie's family had its hands full with her grandfather, who had gotten a shotgun and some buckshot:

"The idea," said Grandma, "of his wanting to fight the whole Home Guard with one old shotgun and he never could kill anything when he went hunting! Never killed anything in his life!"

"Now Grandma," said Jimmie, " you know he killed two squirrels once at one shot."

"Yes once and that was an accident—that was the only time."

For Lizzie Hardin the high point of the war—and perhaps of her whole life—was the arrival of Morgan and his dashing troops in Harrodsburg. But waving their handkerchiefs and throwing flowers at Morgan's men, as well as outspokenly supporting the Confederate cause, brought trouble to Lizzie, Jimmie, and their mother.

In July, 1862, the military governor of Kentucky sent out orders "to fit up quarters for the imprisonment of such disloyal females" throughout the state as the provost marshals thought necessary to arrest. The Hardins were later described by a former marshal as "notorious and babbling rebels." Although they were warned that they might be arrested, the Hardins refused to leave town and pushed local authorities into arresting them, thus making them martyrs.

An interesting example of the slave-mistress relationship occurred as Lizzie Hardin left for jail. Her slave, Lottie, sought her out: "Yes, Miss Lizzie, I'm come to tell you good-bye 'cause you ain't got no sense." Not angered in the least, Lizzie laughed at Lottie's view—which seems accurate enough.

Eventually the Hardin women were banished from Kentucky and sent South, spending the rest of the war in Georgia. When fighting was desperate in 1864, Lizzie Hardin helped nurse sick and wounded soldiers at a Marietta hospital. Though she gives no account of this experience, it must have taught her that war was far from the romantic conflict she had first imagined.

The bitter division among Kentuckians is exemplified in the unfortunate Mary Todd Lincoln. Loyal to her husband and the Union, she was suspected of favoring the Confederacy. Of those surviving among her father's fourteen children, only she, a brother, and a half-sister supported the Union. Her other brother and three half-brothers joined the Confederate army, and three half-sisters were married to Confederate officers. As Northern newspapers were fond of pointing out, she had eleven second cousins in the Carolina Light Dragoons.

As a young woman in Lexington, Mary Todd had tried to conceal her scholarly interests from local beaux. Lincoln, however, liked talking with her about serious subjects. Of this exchange, she wrote a cousin: "I know his intellect, for I've helped to stock it with facts." But a president's wife was supposed to smile and be silent, and as a controversial first lady, she failed to conceal her outspoken impulsiveness and her intelligence.

Her life with its many sorrows is well known. After a century, best sellers and dramas have brought her the understanding denied her during her unhappy lifetime.

No one loved power better than she did, but Mary Todd Lincoln took the traditional route to it—that of a woman's influence over a successful husband. As for other women, if they got the vote, she said, they would "behave in so inconsequent a manner as to reduce the whole matter to an absurdity." In spite of her own ambitious nature, she opposed the suffrage movement.

On the day Lincoln was elected, Lizzie Hardin would have voted against him if she could have. In her journal, she remarked that "having only the boy's privilege of 'hollering' for my candidate, and being denied even that, except in very secluded situations, I determined to leave the country in the hands of the men and take a ramble over the hills."

Lizzie Hardin understood the trade-off implicit in her position. Five years later, on their way home to Kentucky through conquered Georgia, the male members of her party had to make a fire, keep it going all night, and watch the baggage in the street. As for the women, "*We* had nothing to do but to sleep [on the floor]. . . . It is a right good thing to be a lady, though it is tolerably tiresome too sometimes."

But the war had profoundly changed the position of women. In a world no longer based on slave labor, the social hierarchy was shaken. Not only were black women freed, but traditional restraints on all women were weakened. Kentucky women were still denied higher education, vocations, and the ballot. But many who, before the war, would have been restricted like Lizzie Hardin to the "tolerably tiresome" life of a lady, would leave the confines of their homes to enter the struggle for these opportunities. At another economic level, many more, out of necessity, would add to the burden of household chores long hours of work in fields and factories.

5

THE WORKERS

*[In] one pickle and preserve factory . . . about 100 young
girls are working for 14 hours a day, six days in the week.*
Investigator's report, 1911

UNNOTICED BY MOST Kentuckians, by the turn of the
century 44,518 "females over ten years of age" were employed by Kentucky industries. Most of these women
worked in Louisville, the most industrialized city in the
largely agricultural state. Always paid less than men in the
same occupations, women in Louisville factories earned an
average of sixty-seven cents a day in 1887 and eighty-seven
cents a day in 1903. In the sewing trades, wages were even
lower.

A powerless class, women workers were not only paid
poorly but also exploited in other ways. Since the 1880s,
men's unions had pushed for the eight-hour day, and by the
early years of the century, most men worked no longer than
ten hours. But many Kentucky women were working days
of twelve, thirteen, and fourteen hours. As unskilled labor,
women worked under the worst of conditions, especially in
the tobacco factories. Observing these women in 1899, a
writer for the Louisville *Courier-Journal* called them
"coarse, ignorant and filthy."

Most male unions excluded women, although a few permitted women to join if they worked at the same wages as
men did—an unusual situation. Women did have some
unions of their own. Herbert Finch, a student of the period,
notes that women workers in Louisville woolen mills joined

the Weavers' Union in a body in 1885, and that women's unions existed in binderies, garment factories, and the millinery trade. But the very fact that these unions were made up entirely of women indicates their lack of strength. Men's unions drew their gradually growing strength from skilled workers, in demand. But women did not share in this accumulating power.

It may be, as some suggest, that factory women in Louisville had little interest in unions. It seems likely, however, that their long hours, to which the burden of household chores must be added, left them little time or strength for organizing.

Two significant incidents in 1893—a depression year—indicate that women felt more loyalty to the union movement than the unions did to women. The previous year, some women laundry workers in Louisville were able to organize a small union called the Laundry Girls' Union, and to negotiate a profit-sharing contract with one laundry. During 1893, when the railroad union was out on strike, the railroads hired "scab" workers to break the strike. When the strikebreakers' clothing was brought to the laundry, the members of the Laundry Girls' Union refused to wash it. In the midst of a depression, these anonymous women quit their jobs rather than support strikebreakers.

Yet in the same year, a Louisville union organizer, E. L. Cronk of the American Federation of Labor, complained that women who took jobs as clerks and bookkeepers created unemployment for men. At the expense of women workers, Cronk repeated the old management excuse for underpaying women: most women were only working for "spending money," not to support families. If anyone actually believed that a woman would work in a laundry or tobacco redryer eleven or twelve hours a day, six days a week, as a hobby, the investigations of the twentieth century disproved this rationalization. Whether or not Cronk himself believed his statement, it is clear that the labor organizer's interest lay with men workers, to the detriment of women.

In the 1880s, two women labor leaders came to Louisville

to speak to mass meetings of men and women. They were Fanny Allyn of Cincinnati and Leonora M. Barry of New York. An eloquent speaker, Leonora Barry had quickly moved from a stocking factory to a leading position in the Knights of Labor. But in 1889, the year she spoke in Louisville, she reported to the Knights that throughout the country, women's response to labor organizing was disappointing. The reasons she gave were the women workers' ignorance, apathy, and

the habit of submission and acceptance without question of any terms offered them, with the pessimistic view of life in which they see no ray of hope. [They] cannot be said to live, as living means the enjoyment of nature's gifts, but they simply vegetate like partially petrified creatures. . . . Again, many women are deterred from joining labor organizations . . . foolishly imagining that with marriage their connection with and interest in labor matters end; often finding, however, that their struggle has only begun when they have to go back to the shop for two instead of one. All this is the results or effects of the environments and conditions surrounding women in the past and present, and can be removed only by constant agitation and education.

Such was her view of women whom the *Courier-Journal* writer would see only as "coarse, ignorant and filthy." The following year, Leonora Barry resigned her position, and the disintegrating Knights of Labor gave up on the organization of women.

In the new century, others—mostly women—became concerned about the exploitation of women by industry. Out of the settlement-house movement in Chicago grew a proposal to engage expert investigators, federally funded, to examine factory conditions for both women and children. An interesting combination of organizations helped push this bill through Congress. Made up principally of women, these organizations included church and civic groups, the Women's Trade Union League, and—as evidence of growing activism on the part of formerly social organizations— the General Federation of Women's Clubs. As a result of their efforts, nineteen volumes were prepared by experts and funded by Congress from 1908 to 1911.

A lightly industrialized state, Kentucky was not included in these investigations. But they made an impact on some women with civic concerns, particularly in Louisville, where a Consumers League had been formed and where most Kentucky industry was centered. These women were aware, too, that one of the originators of the national investigation plan was a Kentuckian, the brilliant Sophonisba Breckinridge of the University of Chicago. A Lexington native, she had many active ties with Kentucky.

Deciding to engage an investigator from Chicago and to pay for his services through private contributions, the Consumers League of Louisville asked the governor to appoint a commission "for the purpose of investigating the conditions of working women in Kentucky in industrial establishments." The League's concerns took on added urgency when, on March 25, 1911, in New York City, the famous Triangle Shirtwaist Company fire killed 146 workers, mostly women and girls, who died in large part because of the company's indifference to fire protection. That month the governor appointed the commission, made up mostly of Louisville women. Its goal was to get out its report before the Kentucky legislature met the following January.

Behind the whole enterprise was the driving force of Frances Ingram, head resident of Neighborhood House, a settlement house in Louisville. "Without her counsel and guidance," wrote the Chicago investigator, S. M. Hartzmann, "the investigator . . . might have been at a loss as to what he should do, especially during the first month of his work."

During the rest of 1911, at the new commission's direction, Hartzmann investigated the condition of women workers in 186 Kentucky factories, employing 11,048 women, or about one-fourth of the women workers in the state. Using Louisville prices to estimate the weekly wage a woman would need to support herself, the commission arrived at $6.50 as a bare minimum:

The sum of $6.50 is taken because it is believed that a woman who must support herself cannot provide food, lodging, clothes and washing on less than that sum. Careful estimates of the lowest cost at which working girls can obtain necessaries in Louisville are as follows:

Board and Lodging	$4.00	per week
Clothes and Shoes	1.40	per week
Car Fare	.60	per week
Laundry	.50	per week
TOTAL	$6.50	per week

This allows nothing for illness, recreation, or ribbons.

It also allowed nothing for savings toward old age, and old women had no alternative but to work on as long as they could. In fact, few Kentucky women earned $6.50 a week, and many earned far less. The estimated average for Kentucky women workers was $5.96 a week. In its report, the commission observed: "It is a matter of common knowledge that wages of $5.96 per week will hardly keep the body and soul of the worker together, but it is a matter of equally common knowledge that many of these women receiving this wage or less have children, parents or other dependents to support in addition to themselves."

With candor, the report faced other problems of women workers:

The lives of working women in Kentucky are daily threatened by the total absence of fire escapes, or by structures that are in themselves death traps. Their health is menaced by insufficient light and ventilation, by the failure to provide seats and by long hours of work. Their morals are attacked not alone by the disregard of common decencies in the provision of toilets insufficiently, or not at all, separated from those for men, but especially by the payment of insufficient wages, which must in many cases be supplemented from other sources.

From prostitution, in other words.

Of prostitution, the report spoke euphemistically:

The factories in which very much complaint was made with regard to unsteadiness and improper conduct of girls are precisely those where the hours of work were the longest, sanitary conditions and wages unsatisfactory. As one general manager expressed it: "And strangest of all, the girls who lead improper lives outside of the factory are precisely those that receive the lowest wages."

An offender on all counts—wages, hours, working conditions—was the tobacco industry, the major employer of women in Kentucky. There the average pay was only $4.62 a week, the normal workday was ten hours, and the normal week sixty hours. Lack of ventilation threatened health, as in some factories all windows were closed because air would dry out the tobacco leaf. The factories were full of dust:

When a worker is bent over her work for ten hours a day stripping tobacco leaf of its stem at her highest speed, she will certainly produce some dust. Consequently, in the larger factories where many women are engaged in this process, the air is laden with tobacco dust. Where stemming is done by means of machinery, the quantity of dust is still greater.

But the tobacco industry claimed that these conditions were harmless and might even be good for the workers: "employers claim that tobacco is 'a good disinfectant' and not especially injurious to health."

After the tobacco industry, the clothing industry was the largest employer of women in Kentucky. Here the hours were even longer:

In some establishments they work overtime at a rate of three hours per day, every day in the week, in addition to the regular ten-hour day. The longest work-day is, therefore, thirteen hours, from 7 o'clock in the morning to 9 o'clock in the evening, with but two half-hour intervals for rest and lunch.

In addition, clothing was seasonal work, with months of layoffs during which women had no pay at all.

Wages in the clothing industry were based on piecework, "the most unsatisfactory of all methods of paying for labor." Piecework taught only "an infinitesimal part of the trade, such as sewing in sleeves" and was "extremely tiresome and

72

exhausting." Setting a rate based on the work of "some un-
usually quick, healthy, energetic and highly efficient worker" who would earn five, six, or seven dollars a week, the
companies kept the average worker at a very low wage—
starting at two dollars a week.

In mills, long hours were again the rule:

5 days in the week employees are working about 11 hours per day,
and on Saturdays only 5 or 6 hours. Thus the normal work-day in
the mills is about one hour longer than the customary work-day in
other employments, from 6:30 in the morning to 6:00 in the evening, with but 20 to 40 minutes for rest and lunch. . . . In addition
to the regular hours of work, three of the nine mills visited reported overtime work for 2 1/2 to 3 1/2 hours per evening, four
evenings a week, for two to six months in the year.

In addition to the fourteen-and-a-half-hour day, women
mill workers had to endure a high level of noise and "a constant temperature of about 90° and a humidity of 80. The
windows are therefore closed for the most part and lint and
hemp fill the over-heated and vitiated atmosphere of the
mill." And pay was low, about $3.50 a week, "while in the
largest mill in the State 'the young girls are paid 40 cents a
day, or $2.40 a week, though there are not over 30 or 40
girls whose wages do not exceed $3.00 a week.' "

In "Dry Goods and 5 and 10 Cent Stores," workers at
least had decent lighting and ventilation, but they had to
stand all day, and the hours were long:

The hours of work are, as a rule, from 8 a.m. to 5:30 p.m. in the
summer months, and to 6 p.m. the rest of the year. Some of the
stores are open till 10 o'clock on Saturdays, while in one town
(Covington) they are usually open till 9 o'clock in the evening on
Mondays and till 10 on Saturdays. Likewise on holidays, such as
the 4th of July, Thanksgiving, etc., most of the stores are open in
the forenoon at least. About Christmas time, all stores, excepting
one, are open till 10 o'clock in the evening from four days to three
weeks before Christmas. . . . The employees are never paid for
overtime work, but occasionally they are given a Christmas present in one or another store.

Nearly half of all such clerks averaged only $3.95 a week, and wages started at two dollars a week.

When telephone exchanges were first established, in the 1880s, operators were men. Since the pay was "incredibly low" and opportunities for advancement nonexistent, men abandoned these jobs and thus women fell heir to them. By 1911 in Kentucky, all operators were women—and all young women, the belief being that only young women had the alertness and agility for the job.

More than half of all telephone operators in Kentucky made less than six dollars a week in 1911, and their hours were poor. Often they had to work a split shift that made them come to work twice a day, in the mornings and again in the evenings. Usually they worked nine or ten hours a day and at least every other Sunday, and for Sundays they got no additional pay. In some Kentucky towns, operators had to work three out of every four Sundays, and even on their only Sunday off they could be required to fill in as replacement.

Night operators had no difficulty keeping track of their nights off duty. They had none. As the commission reported, "excepting two or three exchanges, the night operators are on duty every night, and are never off."

Moreover, the telephone companies worked out an interesting rationalization for failing to pay night operators for all the hours they worked. In most exchanges, night operators worked twelve or thirteen hours and were paid for only ten. Their employers reasoned "that at night time there is not much work, and the girls can sleep two or three hours." The commission observed: "There were no accommodations for sleeping purposes." Thus these women could sleep, if they could do so sitting up and wearing heavy headsets. And for two or three hours of work a night, they were not paid.

In laundries, women did not fare as badly as the commission had expected. Whether or not the Laundry Girls' Union of the 1890s had any long-term effect on the industry is not possible to surmise, but laundries, at least in Louisville, did

Women office workers

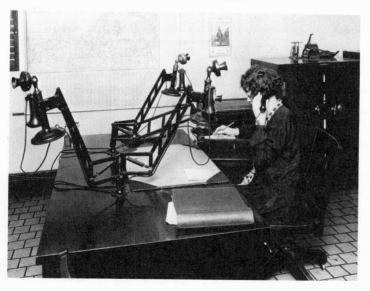

Night telephone operator

not live up to their bad reputations. The investigator found it heartening to report that the "hours of work never exceed 55 hours per week." Moreover, most workers were paid five or six dollars a week, only slightly below the minimum needed to sustain life. Many had an unusual privilege: Saturdays off, managed by working until nine or ten o'clock on Friday nights.

Conditions were less sanguine in some other industries, such as

one pickle and preserve factory where about 100 young girls are working for 14 hours a day, six days in the week, for about four months in the year, while in the slack season, part of the force are laid off. In addition to this, sanitary conditions are unsatisfactory, and the wages not especially encouraging.

Dangers to health and safety abounded. In one tile factory that used red and white lead,

. . . notwithstanding the reputation of the factory for its cases of lead-poisoning, as well as the unusual unsteadiness of the labor force,—notwithstanding all this, the ventilation in the factory is altogether insufficient, and the washing facilities very inadequate. Only a hydrant and sink is provided; no soap or towels. Accordingly most of the employees eat their lunch with soiled and unwashed hands.

Lighting was usually poor in these industries, and toilet facilities unclean, out of order, or nonexistent. At one factory, a single outhouse served a large number of men and women.

Although Kentucky had a law about fire escapes, the law was far from stringent. A metal fire escape was required if a building were three or more stories tall, if the city had more than 10,000 residents, and if more than twenty persons were employed in the building. Even this law was often ignored. The commission cited an example:

The factory is crowded with machinery to an extent that a quick escape in case of fire would be impossible. Still there is only one old and rusty iron ladder on one side of the building, which would scarcely support the weight of an average human being, while the wooden bridge that leads from the window to this shadow of a fire escape is in so dilapidated a condition that it would not be safe to place one foot on it even if the greatest care were exercised.

To get firsthand information for the commission, Ruth Sapinsky of Neighborhood House got a job in a Louisville factory shelling nuts, mostly pecans, at piece wages. For three nine-hour days, pausing only twenty minutes for lunch, she worked as hard and as fast as she could. Her total earnings came to thirty-seven and a half cents.

Of her 200 fellow workers, few earned much:

Mrs. J., a pathetic old lady, who sat across from me and who had been working a month, was even slower than I; the smartest girl in the factory, who had been there some five years and had reached the enviable wages of six and seven dollars each week, had only made thirteen cents a day as a beginner. . . . I found three dollars to be the average wage throughout the factory.

But these earnings included night work as well as day work. To make that much, the women took baskets of nuts home at quitting time. After a nine-hour day, almost every employee had to spend her evenings shelling nuts. Thus their lives were rounds of endless work.

These pecans went to confectioners and "fancy grocers" who catered to the rich. The commission members—many of whom belonged to the latter category—were shocked at another item in Ruth Sapinsky's report: the women also had to sweep up shells from the floor at night, and having no dust pans, they *used the same tins in which they kept their nuts during the day as dust pans.*" Thus the community's health, too, was jeopardized by indifference to sanitation.

Throughout the report, Hartzmann and the commission emphasized that workers who are not sick and exhausted turn out more work. Not all factories were offenders, and appealing to the profit motive of owners and managers, the commission quoted several employers who operated safe, clean factories as saying: "It pays to treat your employees well." Although employees were paid nothing for overtime work, "It does not pay" to work them overtime, these model employers were quoted as concluding.

But the commission understood that industrial conditions could be changed only by legislative action, not by example, and the body proposed a number of reforms to the 1912 legislature. These included the appointment of two women as assistants to the State Labor Inspector, to help enforce existing laws on child labor and fire escapes; a law to require separate, and clean, toilets, for both sexes; a law to require seats for women employees, and the appointment of an unpaid commission to investigate and propose a law regulating ventilation and sanitation in industry, and to examine the question of minimum wages for women and minors. Most important, the commission urged the legislature to limit work hours to nine a day and fifty-four a week—hours already on the books in such labor states as New York and Massachusetts. In fact, the eight-hour day was already law in Washington and California.

All they got, however, from the 1912 legislature was an act limiting the work of women in industry to ten hours a day and sixty hours a week—a disappointing conclusion.

But these women in the Consumers League and the investigative commission had tried to call attention to the lot of their powerless sisters. That they failed is not surprising, given industry's economic interest in maintaining a large pool of marginally compensated workers, and given, too, the indifference of the legislature and the public, and the hopelessness of the women workers themselves. Like Leonora Barry, Hartzmann and the commission members noted the women's stoic acceptance of any conditions. The report observed that when recently hired women were asked how much they earned, they often replied, "I do not know." As an explanation, the report offered: "That women in industry do not bargain with their employers for wages, but are glad to 'get a job' and leave the question of wages to the discretion of the employer." Women placed little value on themselves.

In another area, the commission's report was less than perceptive. Perhaps because the investigator was male and the women supporting the investigation were well-to-do, the report does not point out the additional hardship of household chores in the lives of working women. After an exhausting day of ten to fourteen hours in a poorly ventilated, dirty factory, a woman would make her way home on foot or by streetcar, to face washing, cooking, and cleaning. Physically demanding in themselves, these chores had to be performed without any "conveniences." These women cooked on woodburning stoves, built their own fires, made their own soap, washed with a washboard and tub, baked their own bread. In Victorian England, one of the arguments against women in factories was that their children were often unsupervised, dirty, and ill fed. The realistic reply was that unless these women worked, their children would not be fed at all.

A decade later, in 1921, another report on women in Kentucky industries was carried out entirely by women. Requested by the Kentucky Federation of Women's Clubs, the investigation was made by women agents of the Women's Bureau of the U.S. Department of Labor. The bureau had just been established in 1920, partly through the persistent pressure of the Women's Trade Union League. The climate created by the success of the women's suffrage movement also played a part in the bureau's creation. Surprisingly, the new Women's Bureau was headed by a woman with first-hand experience in factory labor and union organizing, Mary Anderson, a former worker in a shoe factory and leader of the WTUL.

In Kentucky, the agents had the cooperation of "a number of women's organizations. . . . Among these were . . . the League of Women's Voters, the Consumers League, and the Young Women's Christian Association."

Published in 1923, the report revealed few significant

changes since the 1911 report. In the decade that included World War I, wages had gone up for Kentucky women workers to a median of $10.75 for white women and $8.35 for black women. But prices had risen sharply. As for hours, the bureau reported:

Kentucky is one of the backward States in regard to hour legislation for women. It permits a 10-hour day and a 60-hour week. It has no law prohibiting night work for women and no law requiring one day of rest in seven . . . a large proportion of the women were working under hour schedules sufficiently long to be a decided menace not only to the health of the women themselves but to their efficient employment in industry and the well-being of the community.

Moreover, the women investigators added that "women wage earners frequently are home makers as well; that many of them look after families and perform home duties before and after the hours spent in industrial plants."

Occupational hazards were still plentiful. The specific, detailed accounts of these dangers indicate that the women investigators were effective interviewers and had practical experience in factories:

Several women were working on unguarded presses and cutters. A considerable number of women in laundries were working on machines where there was danger of burns as well as of getting caught in the presses. . . . In one factory a group of women on painting machines stood all day directly over the fumes, as the machines had no exhausts. . . . A number of women who worked in a box factory complained . . . that the glue used had some ingredient which ate into their hands until they bled. Others told of the cuts and scratches from dry tobacco, and another group of the splinters that they got into their hands when they polished furniture.

Less obvious problems also caught the agents' eyes:

Many tobacco plants made no effort to provide seats or workbenches. In most cases the tobacco was piled on the floor, and the women sat on improvised benches, boxes, or stools to sort or stem it. They often sat astride the bench, and they rarely had any support for their backs. . . . Moreover, most of the stools or benches had to be so low in order that the women could reach the tobacco that the workers were forced to sit all day with their legs stretched out straight before them. All these women worked under great strain due to their cramped, unnatural positions; yet this arrangement was unnecessary.

Insanitary conditions were still prevalent. Drinking facilities could easily spread disease:

The common cup which has been universally condemned was found in 39 establishments. Several of the workrooms in various plants had as their only supply of drinking water a pail which was filled with water in the morning. Many workers had to go long distances for a drink.

Few plants—and only two of the twelve investigated that dealt with food—provided sanitary washing facilities:

A common description . . . of the facilities furnished was an iron sink, a single coldwater faucet, and no soap or towels. In a few plants a tin pail or basin was the only place where washing was possible.

Toilets were dirty, unventilated, and inadequate—in some cases, one toilet for sixty or sixty-five women. And "in one large plant . . . the women had to walk down an outside flight of stairs and then go nearly a block to an outside toilet." As the ultimate in indifference, "Two establishments visited during the Kentucky survey had no toilets whatsoever for their employees."

Most Kentucky factories provided no lunch rooms, or rooms that were dirty, too close to toilets, or too crowded:

In tobacco plants and in laundries, where the nature of women's work is such that they operate all day under unpleasant conditions due to fumes and dust or humidity, most of the women had to eat lunch in the workrooms. . . . since most of them were piece workers they never left their work benches at lunch time, but stopped only long enough to eat a sandwich.

In addition to health hazards, fire hazards were the rule rather than the exception, and Kentucky factory owners violated existing fire laws at will, as they had a decade earlier.

Oddly, the Women's Bureau passed along with approval a strange, but not uncommon, notion that had appeared in a report on the telephone industry in New York:

the years 16 to 23 are those during which the nervous and physical system of a woman is peculiarly sensitive to strain and susceptible to injury. Injury sustained at this time of life is apt to be more far-reaching than would be the effects from similar causes in maturer years.

Other myths, however, the investigators took pains to dispel:

The theory that women who live with their families do not need such high wages as do those living away from home is not only fallacious but extremely vicious, since unscrupulous employers offer it as an excuse for low pay. Obviously a working girl's family should not be expected to subsidize industry. Furthermore, definite proof has been furnished that women who live at home have heavy financial responsibilities. They frequently must support not only themselves but dependents as well.

Although working widows were generally accepted as having to support their children, employers encouraged the notion that married women were only working for "pin money." The investigators called this idea a "pet but false" theory, and reported: "Interviews with Kentucky women at work in stores, mills, and factories furnished additional evidence that women with husbands are working outside the home to help in the actual maintenance of the family."

Advocating shorter hours and adequate pay, the U.S. Women's Bureau report described the average income of a Kentucky working woman as "so meager. . . . covering bare living expenses" that it was impossible to save for old age or illness.

Sixteen years later, in 1937, the League of Women Voters

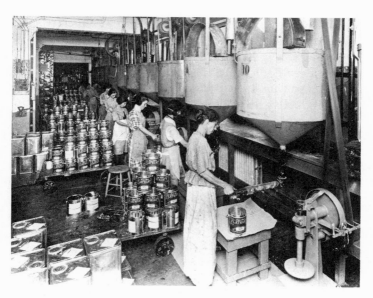

Women factory workers in Louisville

Dime-store clerks

in Louisville asked for another survey by the Women's Bureau. More Kentucky women were working—146,678, according to the 1930 census—but Kentucky law still permitted a ten-hour day and a sixty-hour week. Few women still worked that long, perhaps because industries were not fully productive during the depression. For all Kentucky industry, women's average earnings in 1937 were $13 a week.

The 1937 report observed what had always been true: that black women were worse off than any other group. Not only were their wages low, but they were also restricted to certain kinds of factory work, such as poultry-dressing. The investigators noted that "the figures serve to emphasize the lack of opportunities for employment of Negro women in the manufacturing industries of Kentucky."

No investigation could be made of black women as telephone operators and dime-store clerks, jobs that however poorly paid and however long the hours, were more desirable than factory work because they were less dangerous and dirty. Black women were excluded from such work. They would continue to be shut out until federal civil rights legislation was passed three decades later.

As women entered the blue-collar work force, they also began moving into white-collar jobs—again, at the lowest level of pay. In Louisville, when American Federation of Labor organizer Cronk complained in 1893 that women were taking jobs that should belong to men as bookkeepers and clerks, he provided evidence that a new group of women workers was beginning to develop.

When the commercial typewriter came into use in the 1870s, most "typewriters," as the operators were called, were men. As employers found that women could do the same work and would do it for much less, often half of what men received, they began hiring women for most low-level office jobs. Nationally, by 1900, women made up 75.7 percent of all stenographers and typists, 12.9 percent of all clerks and copyists, and 28.9 percent of all bookkeepers and accountants. Gradually, some women made their way into positions of more responsibility, although often without the title or salary to match the job.

Louisville newspapers in the nineteenth century carried notices of meetings of businesswomen's clubs, often announcing some project in self-improvement for the year— learning French, for example. Their goals seemed more educational and social than economic or political.

During World War I, when women's groups were being organized to support the war, the national YWCA called a meeting of career women in business and the professions, and asked a Kentucky woman to head the group. She was Lena Madesin Phillips, an honor graduate of the University of Kentucky law college and a lawyer practicing in Nicholasville. After the war, the group became the National Federation of Business and Professional Women's Clubs, which chose the slogan: "Equal Pay for Equal Work."

Unequal pay was openly advocated for another group of women entering the work force: schoolteachers. Poorly paid, in rural counties they boarded in "teacherages," were required by their communities to live ascetic lives, and often taught in one-room schools up isolated hollows. As late as 1935, the Bureau of School Service of the College of Education of the University of Kentucky recommended publicly that men be paid more than women teachers, to encourage men into public-school education. This policy was stated by education professionals, the men who influenced decisions in Kentucky schools. Although the suffragist Laura Clay was eighty-six years old at the time, as Paul E. Fuller has noted, the recommendation was too much for her. She fired a parting shot at the educational establishment, saying that it would be a travesty for injustice to prevail where citizenship was supposedly taught. Equal pay for equal work, the old feminist demanded.

Not only did the post-Civil War years bring women into teaching and office work, and by the thousands, into factories, but also a combination of circumstances brought more women into the fields. A new strain of tobacco, white burley, was introduced in 1864 and soon was on its way to becoming Kentucky's principal money crop. At the same time, slavery was ending.

Tobacco requires much hand labor. Before the war, on large farms, tobacco had been a smaller crop, and black men did most of this work, women helping out occasionally. After slaves were freed, poor white families took their places as tenants working on shares. Owning no land, these tenants had low social status—so low that an appeal for money for a Kentucky mountain institution emphasized that mountain people are "not the 'poor whites,' but self-respecting land-holders." For years at the mercy of both owners and tobacco companies, many tenants were never able to work their way free of debt. It was not until the large migrations to cities that the lot of the remaining tenant farmers, now in short supply, improved.

Among these tenants, women worked along with men in such drudgery as suckering and stripping tobacco. And for the women, field and barn work did not replace household chores but served, instead, as additional burdens. The hardships of poor tenant-farm women were increased by re-peated childbirth. Such women aged early.

Edith Summers Kelley, who had experienced tenant life, wrote articulately of the hard lives of these women in a novel, *Weeds*, published in 1923. A graduate in modern languages of the University of Toronto, Edith Summers had written for newspapers and magazines in New York. She became the secretary of Upton Sinclair and the fiancée of Sinclair Lewis, but she married a poet, Lewis's roommate from Yale. Separating from the poet, she entered a common-law marriage with a sculptor. He had lived on a farm, and when he could not earn a living sculpting, they turned to farming and moved to Scott County, Kentucky, for three years.

A tenant's wife herself, Edith Summers Kelley describes a Kentucky tenant house in winter:

The loose-fitting window sashes rattled, the doors stirred uneasily. The bits of old rag carpet laid upon the floor rose in waves as the wind billowed under them. . . . The wind fluttered the towels over the wash bench and rattled the saucepans that hung on the wall beside the stove. . . . The water bucket was frozen. The milk in the pans was crusted with ice. Cold boiled potatoes left over from the day before were frozen into rocks and eggs were cracked open. The slop bucket on the floor in the corner was frozen solid and the bucket sprung from the force of the expanding ice.

If tobacco represented weeds, so did tenant children. A rural Kentucky schoolroom offers little hope for the future:

Here Lena Moss, an anemic little girl of eighteen, still a child herself in mind and body, who had been educated for a year and a half in the Georgetown High School, did what she could to drill the three R's. . . . Lena's pupils were mostly inbred and undernourished children, brought up from infancy on skim milk, sowbelly, and cornmeal cakes. . . . They were pallid, long-faced, adenoidal little creatures, who were too tired after the long walk to school to give the teacher much trouble.

At a country square dance in central Kentucky, the celebrants show the effect of their harsh lives:

The older women, exhorted by their daughters and husbands, were at last persuaded to forsake their chairs and join the circle. Although nearly all of the "old folks" were under fifty and most of them in the thirties and forties, it was a scarecrow array of bent limbs, bowed shoulders, sunken chests, twisted contortions, and jagged angularities, that formed the circle for the old folks' dance. Grotesque in their deformities, these men and women, who should have been in the full flower of their lives, were already classed among the aged. And old they were in body and spirit. . . . The skinny, dried-up, little women in their black dresses did not get much enjoyment out of the dance. There was neither lure nor mystery about the other sex for them any more. . . . They went through the dance as they had gone through everything else since childhood, as a matter of course, because the circumstances of their lives demanded it of them.

Later in the novel, when tobacco companies rig prices, the novel's protagonists lose a year's work and are caught in a cycle of debt—a cycle from which they will never escape.

In a letter printed in a Kentucky student magazine, *The Transylvanian*, in 1924, Mrs. Kelley wrote that she and her husband had lived "about twenty miles from Georgetown, and about eleven from Sadieville." As for

conditions in the tobacco growing industry, I have been told that it is considerably better now than it used to be. However, the conditions which I have described were absolutely true in Scott County during 1912, '13, and '14, during which years my husband and I lived there and my husband grew tobacco.

She admitted that "I have not painted a very enticing picture of Kentucky life," but she said: "I know my section of the state, although it is the only section that I know at all."

The Kelleys tried farming in other places "with indifferent success," she observed, and finally settled in California, where she continued to write. Despite good reviews, *Weeds* was not financially successful. In the late 1930s, Edith Summers Kelley was doing daywork as a maid, and she died in obscurity in the late 1950s. Twenty years later, her novel was rediscovered, and her voice—speaking for the silent—told another generation about the lives of Kentucky tenant women.

While thousands of Kentucky women worked through years of drudgery on farms and in factories, a more fortunate few spent their lives trying to improve conditions for all women. Born to ease and position, though not to power, these women rejected their restricted traditional lives to work for reforms for the powerless. Some thought the ballot was an end in itself; others thought it merely a beginning.

6

THE REFORMERS

Kentucky women are not idiots—even though they are closely related to Kentucky men.
Madeline McDowell Breckinridge, 1915

IN THE FLOWER-DECKED drawing room at "Ashland," on the day after Kentucky ratified the women's suffrage amendment, a receiving line greeted a large crowd of well-groomed guests fortunate enough to receive a coveted invitation. The guest of honor at the venerable home of Henry Clay was none other than Emmeline Pankhurst, English militant—occasionally violent—suffrage leader, who had been beaten, stoned, egged by mobs, many times imprisoned and forcibly fed in English jails. In Mrs. Pankhurst's long campaign of civil disobedience, she herself had smashed windows and thrown rocks, and with her encouragement her followers had burned buildings and lumberyards, cut telegraph and telephone lines, set fire to mailboxes, poured acid on golf greens, sailed over London in a balloon tossing out suffrage pamphlets, and shouted "Votes for Women" through a megaphone at King George V from a box at the opera. Some planted amateur bombs near the Bank of England; one struck Winston Churchill (lightly) with a riding crop, and another leaped to her death in front of the King's horse during the English Derby. Yet in Lexington, on January 7, 1920, the solidly conservative Bluegrass establishment turned out to do Mrs. Pankhurst honor.

Elsewhere in the country, fear of social change ran high. The Lexington *Herald* reported that "Big Jim Larkin, Liverpool dock strike leader now fomenting trouble in America," had spoken at a huge rally held by the Communist Labor Party in New York City, to the alarm of the government. A large-scale Red scare had led to the imprisonment on Ellis Island of 700 suspected Bolsheviks, the *Herald* reported in banner headlines, and warrants were out for 600 more. Nor were the Socialists faring well in the usual postwar political repression. Big Bill Haywood of the IWW had surrendered the day before in Chicago, the Lexington paper noted with evident relief.

But at "Ashland," far from the unkempt Big Jim and Big Bill, the scene was peaceful. Flowers and plants brightened the rooms that January afternoon, and the tea table held poinsettias in a silver pitcher.

"It was a great pleasure to all the guests, who numbered about one hundred and fifty ladies and gentlemen, to see the old home of Henry Clay," wrote the *Herald* society editor, "and to be present for such a happy affair."

A lady herself, whose charm and beauty were most useful to her cause, Mrs. Pankhurst had rubbed elbows with thieves and prostitutes during her many terms in English jails. On this day, however, her colleagues in the receiving line were the officers of the Fayette Equal Rights Association, soon to become the League of Women Voters, and the Women's Club of Central Kentucky.

During the militant phase of the English suffrage movement, from 1902 until 1914, when Mrs. Pankhurst suspended militancy for the duration of the war, more than 1,000 English suffragists had been imprisoned. Mrs. Pankhurst herself had suffered incredible physical hardships. Early, she had grasped the political impact of the hunger strike—a lesson that Gandhi put to use later in India—and the even more terrible thirst strike. English authorities had punitively subjected hunger-striking suffragists to brutal forcible feedings, rubber tubes thrust up the nose and down the throat. A special "Cat and Mouse Act" was passed by Parliament, permitting jailers to release Mrs. Pankhurst or any other hunger striker when she seemed close to death, and to reimprison her as soon as she regained strength. Six times in 1913 alone Mrs. Pankhurst underwent this experience. Traveling with her to Lexington in 1920 was Nurse Pine, who attended her after her many arrests.

At "Ashland," the fare was tea and cakes, said the society editor, who further reported that at her speech that night at the Opera House, Mrs. Pankhurst "wore a graceful gown of black chiffon with jet trimmings." The "orchestra of Kentucky University" played as the well-dressed audience arrived, and the stage was decked with flowers, including "a large bouquet of deep pink roses," presented to Mrs. Pankhurst by the management of the Phoenix Hotel.

Her visit capped a triumph for Kentucky suffragists. On the day before, January 6, the first day of the legislative session, Kentucky ratified the Nineteenth Amendment by an overwhelming vote: 30-8 in the Senate, and 72-25 in the House. The long struggle for the ballot was drawing to a close.

How much the Bluegrass establishment knew about Mrs. Pankhurst was a question. In its announcement of her impending visit, the *Herald* referred only generally to her role in the suffrage movement, and it seems clear that the guests were not all students of the English political scene. "Awfully innocent" is a description of them by a contemporary.

In America, as in England, suffrage was largely an upper-class issue. But in the United States, it was almost always nonviolent. It is true that the American suffragists Alice Paul, Lucy Burns, and many others were jailed, held incommunicado, beaten, forcibly fed, and confined—Miss Burns deprived of clothing—with tubercular and insane inmates. And it is true that they suffered this treatment not for violent acts, but for peaceable picketing in front of the White House in 1917 and 1918.

In Kentucky, however, as in most states, the early suffragists received no ill treatment except ridicule, insult, ostracism, and indifference. As suffrage gained the support of wealthy and influential women—such as Mrs. O. H. P. Belmont of New York and the eccentric Mrs. Frank Leslie, who gave a fortune to the movement—the issue became socially acceptable, even fashionable. So it was in Kentucky, and hence the triumphant occasions at "Ashland" and the Opera House.

Kentucky had no Alice Paul or Emmeline Pankhurst. Always conservative, the state has taken its social reform cautiously and in small doses. Like most Kentuckians, the state's suffragists and other women reformers were essentially conservative: they sought to conserve traditional values by bringing more people into the existing system. Among these women, only Madeline McDowell Breckinridge would have invited Mrs. Pankhurst to Lexington, and only she could have brought off the Pankhurst visit with such élan.

If militant tactics had been useful, she would not have hesitated to use them, according to her sister-in-law, Sophonisba Breckinridge. Nor did she hesitate, as president of the state Equal Rights Association, to bring radical speakers, such as Max Eastman and Charlotte Perkins Gilman, to Kentucky to lecture. A Bluegrass anomaly, she was sympathetic to organized labor and invited Margaret Dreier Robins, president of the National Women's Trade Union League, to visit her in Lexington.

When Mrs. Breckinridge spoke in New York at a meeting on education, one listener, the editor of the New York *Evening Post*, described her as "actuated by a thoroughly militant spirit"—though not of a "lawless" variety—and added that in a political context, she and others "would have been classified as advanced insurgents, because of their interest in social reforms."

Mrs. Breckinridge, of course, did not regard herself as an "insurgent," advanced or otherwise. She had not been much interested in suffrage until she ran into countless political roadblocks that held up reforms. Nor did her guest in 1920, Mrs. Pankhurst, view herself as outside the established order. In her speech at the Lexington Opera House, the English suffragist inveighed against Marxism and warned that "An effort is being made to overthrow every established in-

Madeline McDowell Breckinridge

Sophonisba Breckinridge

stitution in existence." A good many English governmental authorities believed that Mrs. Pankhurst herself had done a great deal to overthrow the old order of things. But in her view, necessary change would strengthen the system.

Mrs. Breckinridge's position in society was unassailable: great-granddaughter of Lucretia Hart and Henry Clay, descendant of Dr. Ephraim McDowell, wife of a Breckinridge. She had an aristocrat's indifference to conformity and at the same time, the charm and intelligence to elicit public support for her undertakings. A vital and imaginative woman, Mrs. Breckinridge might have introduced Big Bill Haywood to Lexington as a visiting Rotarian, had she so desired.

She used her position as well as her ability to lead others in contending with political powers that opposed change. Among her significant accomplishments were a state child labor law (1906) and school attendance laws, a state juvenile court system, tuberculosis sanitoria, a park system in Lexington, playgrounds and a combined model school and settlement house for slum children, as well as the ratification of the suffrage amendment.

To support her reform efforts, Mrs. Breckinridge made astute use of the Lexington *Herald*, of which her husband, Desha, was editor. Writing often for the paper, she broadened the content of the "Woman's Page" to include issues far removed from the usual women's fare—which ran, she claimed, to "ways of making Christmas presents out of old duck skirts . . . 'squaw talk' in short."

Enlisting a new generation of suffrage workers, she characteristically advised them to "get all the fun out of the thing there is in it." And she created entertaining projects, such as group hiking from Covington to Lexington along the railroad, with stops in small towns to campaign for the vote, and automobile tours, with suffrage banners flying.

But she was not as fortunate as she may have seemed. She was physically frail, her life a long struggle with tuberculosis. And although her biographers do not mention it, she had suffered a devastating loss: the amputation of a leg during her girlhood, apparently as the result of an injury and tuberculosis. Nor do they mention that the last years of her short life were darkened by the infidelity of her husband, ironically with another suffragist, in an affair known to many in Lexington as well as to herself. Childless, Mrs. Breckinridge's keen sympathy with children seemed a well-spring for much of her reform work. A favorite poem of hers was Gilman's "Mother to Child": "Thou art one with the rest, I must love thee in them . . . thy mother must dry the tears of the world."

In spite of her physical handicaps, she traveled all over the country speaking for suffrage. On one of these trips in 1915, a Raleigh, North Carolina, newspaper ran an announcement that Mrs. Breckinridge would be met with a brass band and a parade—a joke that greatly distressed Raleigh suffragists. A letter she wrote about this occasion reveals her wit, her forthright attitude toward suffrage tactics, and the conscious use she made of her Kentucky bloodlines:

It was an April Fool joke, but it made the suffragists tear their hair. They are trying to get suffrage there in the most lady-like manner, without having anybody find out they want it. They just had me in the middle of the day like a Lenten service. As I spoke under the portrait of my great-grandfather, and as he had dedicated the capitol in the forties, that lent a little respectability to me and suffrage.

When the occasion called for it, she could be acerbic. In a letter to the governor of Kentucky, who had asked women for large-scale volunteer efforts and otherwise ignored them, she charged him with treating women "as if they were kindergarten children." She told the governor:

Kentucky women are not idiots—even though they are closely related to Kentucky men. . . . Wouldn't it be better . . . to wake up to the fact that women are one-half the people of Kentucky, that neither Kentucky nor the Nation can get along without our help, and hereafter to ask for it on a self-respecting basis?

Mrs. Breckinridge's style, her wit and assurance, were very different from the temperament of the earlier Kentucky suffrage leader, Laura Clay. But the suffrage movement itself had changed greatly over the decades.

When Laura Clay and her sisters—Mary Barr, Annie, and Sallie—began working for women's rights in the 1870s, Kentucky was one of the most backward states in legal rights for women. Always conservative, Kentucky had not shared in the progressive changes made by states to the north and by new states. And since it had not seceded, Kentucky did not undergo the post-Civil War constitutional revisions that improved women's position in conservative ex-Confederate states—particularly Georgia, North Carolina, and South Carolina. Thus Kentucky drifted along in a political backwater.

For example, when all other states permitted a married woman to make a will, Kentucky still denied her this right. If a woman owned property, on her marriage all of it became her husband's, to dispose of as he wished. She owned nothing, not even the clothes she wore. If a husband died, the wife inherited a third of his personalty and a life interest in a third of his real estate. But if a wife died, the husband inherited all of her personalty, and if there were children, a life interest in all of her real estate. She could not make contracts, sue, or be sued. And if she took a job, her husband had the right to collect and spend her wages.

He had the sole right of guardianship over their children, even if she left him, and even over an unborn child. He could separate the children from their mother if he wished, and at his death, he could will their guardianship to some other male. If he did not support his family, that was his business. He was expected to furnish the necessities of life, but as Laura Clay wrote, "If he has only his wages, there is no law to punish him for non-support."

And although widows and unmarried women had to pay taxes, women could not vote. In 1838, Kentucky had been the first state to permit any kind of women's suffrage, however limited. A law allowed widows with school-age children, in country school districts only, to vote for school trustees. In 1888, this law was extended to allow "tax-paying widows and spinsters"—again, only in country districts—to vote on school taxes. Even this very limited suffrage was repealed in 1902. In *The History of Woman Suffrage*, an editor's note comments that the law was repealed "because more colored than white women voted in Lexington at the spring election. This is the only instance where the suffrage has been taken from women after being conferred by a legislature." Thus Kentucky occupies a unique position in the history of suffrage.

Laura Clay had personal experience of the legal position of women in Kentucky. While her father, the famed emancipationist Cassius Clay, remained in Europe for years as ambassador to Russia, her mother improved the Clay estate in Madison County, turning the farm into a profitable enterprise. Born Mary Jane Warfield of a well-to-do Lexington family, Mrs. Clay, during the forty-five years of her marriage, had contributed to "White Hall" her hard work, money, and shrewd management. Eventually, Clay's indiscretions in Europe and the arrival at "White Hall" of a four-year-old Russian boy, his illegitimate son, brought the marriage to the breaking point. With nothing to show for her years of effort, Mrs. Clay returned to Lexington, and Clay later divorced her for desertion. Her family was affluent; otherwise, she would have been penniless under Kentucky law.

All of this had a profound effect on Laura Clay and her sisters, and certainly Cassius Clay's own tyrannical nature must have affected them. In spite of his reputation as an emancipationist, he sold Emily, nurse of his son, Cassius, Jr., and all her family South to work as field hands, on the fantastic claim that she had poisoned the child. This he did despite her acquittal by a Madison County jury for a total lack of evidence to substantiate the charges Clay brought against her.

Moreover, he had a brutal streak of savagery that emerged in his famous knife fights, in which he gouged out eyes and hacked off ears. As for his daughters, Cassius Clay opposed women's rights and higher education for women, and he seemed to take little interest in the intelligent, unusual young women that he had sired.

With their mother, the Clay daughters began their long campaign to improve women's status—a quest that had a religious dimension for them. In letters, Laura Clay wrote, "This work is God's cause, and He is the Leader of all our campaigns." And the story was told in Richmond that when Sallie Clay Bennett wanted to go to a suffrage convention and her husband opposed her going, she came down to breakfast one morning to say that the Lord had spoken to her in the night. In her dream, God told her: "Sister, rise!—and go to the meeting." She went.

As her sisters' families claimed more of their time, the unmarried Laura Clay took on the major responsibilities for the Kentucky Equal Rights Association, serving as its president from its founding in 1888 until 1912. A large, formidable woman with a dogged, somewhat ponderous, style, Miss Clay withstood years of rejection and disappointment in a cause few Kentuckians understood. Florence Shelby Cantrill, Lexington's first woman legislator, remembered Miss Clay as "always very formal," but in her later years an avid bridge player, not devoid of humor: "Miss Laura could laugh." She was also a staunch Episcopalian—unlike her ERA successor, Mrs. Breckinridge, who was a nominal Episcopalian but never attended church—and a supporter of the temperance movement, as were many of the early generation of suffragists.

Little interest in women's suffrage appeared in Kentucky before the Clay sisters took on the cause. In 1853, five years after the first women's rights convention in Seneca Falls, New York, the feminist Lucy Stone spoke in Louisville, and in 1872, the originator of the Seneca Falls convention, Elizabeth Cady Stanton, also spoke there. What probably was the first women's suffrage organization in Kentucky was founded in the village of Glendale, in rural Hardin County, in 1867. But this isolated phenomenon vanished. Neither Lucy Stone nor Elizabeth Cady Stanton lived to cast a ballot, and it is unlikely that any of the anonymous Glendale suffragists did so either.

As early as 1879, Mary Barr Clay arranged for the famous suffragist Susan B. Anthony to speak at Richmond. Paul E. Fuller reports in *Laura Clay and the Woman's Rights Movement* that Miss Anthony made two speeches there, at Green's Opera Hall and the courthouse, impressing the good-sized crowds with her view that the vote was necessary to protect women economically. Mary Jane Warfield Clay described the great suffrage leader as "very pleasant in conversation; a homely woman of sixty years of age, very well satisfied with herself and her doings."

In 1881, the American Woman Suffrage Association, led by Lucy Stone, met in Louisville, and Mary Barr Clay made a speech urging the revision of Kentucky's laws. Two years later, Mary Barr Clay was elected president of the national organization, speaking on suffrage in Washington at a hearing of the House Judiciary Committee in 1884.

The Clay sisters remained close to Susan B. Anthony, and Miss Anthony returned to Kentucky in 1894 with another suffrage leader, Carrie Chapman Catt, to speak at Lexington, Wilmore, Louisville, Owensboro, and Paducah. When Miss Anthony died in 1906, the vote was still fourteen years away. The final victory was masterminded by Mrs. Catt.

Gradually, grudgingly, successes came in Kentucky. In 1894, decades after most states had done so, Kentucky passed a married women's property law and a law permitting married women to make wills. A separate House of Reform for girls "equal to that of boys" was established in 1896, and women were allowed to serve on the board of directors. Women physicians were permitted for women's wards in hospitals for the insane in 1898. In 1900, married women were given the right, at last, to their own earnings. Ten years later, the age of consent—and the age at which Kentucky girls might marry—was raised from twelve to sixteen. And in 1910 a co-guardianship law was passed, finally recognizing the mother's claim to her own child.

But this list gives no indication of the years of fruitless petitioning, letter writing, speechmaking, and the countless disappointments that went into the effort for each reform. In 1890, for example, the Equal Rights Association got 9,000 signatures on petitions asking for property rights for married women. One woman, Mrs. S. M. Hubbard of Hickman, personally collected 2,240 signatures. (Still undiscouraged after twenty-two years, Mrs. Hubbard gave a thousand dollars in 1912 to the impecunious state ERA.) But though the 1890 legislation passed the Senate, it failed in the House.

Again, while the Kentucky constitution was being rewritten in 1890-91, the ERA worked feverishly to get changes beneficial to women. Josephine K. Henry of Versailles spoke eloquently over the state and wrote no fewer than 231 articles for the press: 200 on property rights and thirty-one on suffrage, a ratio reflecting the likelihood of acceptance of the two issues. But women got nothing.

Then, too, the list of successes does not reflect the insults and ridicule heaped on early suffragists by such powerful persons as Henry Watterson, editor of the Louisville *Courier-Journal*. Constantly gibing at Kentucky suffragists, he called them "silly-sallies," "Crazy Janes," and "red-nosed angels."

Oddly, though women could not vote, they were being elected to public office. Four women were elected county school superintendents in 1889, eight in 1893, and eighteen in 1897. In school board elections in 1895, 5,000 women voters turned out in Covington and 2,800 in Newport, but women candidates lost in both cities. However, in Lexington that year, when women candidates were rejected by both Democrats and Republicans, they made up their own "Independent Ticket," including a woman and a man from each ward. Private homes were used for women to register, apparently to avoid the contaminating environs of the county courthouse, and the registration officers were all women.

Front row, from left: Harriet Upton, Dr. Anna Howard Shaw, Susan B. Anthony, Carrie Chapman Catt *Back row:* Kate Gordon, Dr. Cora Smith Eaton, Alice Stone Blackwell, Laura Clay

Voters prepare to cast their first ballots for a president

Moreover, the "Independent Ticket" won—a heartening triumph for suffragists in Lexington, always the suffrage hotbed of the state.

The long struggle had produced hard-won gains, and when the National American Woman Suffrage Association held its national convention in Louisville in 1911, there was much to celebrate. The distinguished women present, and the variety of organizations represented, made it clear that the social isolation of the early suffragists was over. No longer would Laura Clay and a handful of others carry the responsibility alone. As she reported of the convention:

> The College Equal Suffrage League held a business meeting in the Seelbach Hotel . . . followed by a luncheon for college and professional women. The president of the League, Dr. M. Carey Thomas, president of Bryn Mawr College, was toast mistress and Dr. [Anna Howard] Shaw and Miss Jane Addams were guests of honor. . . .
>
> Professor Sophonisba Breckinridge . . . of Chicago University, considered with keen analysis woman suffrage in its relation to the interests of the wage-earning women.

Among the organizations represented were such disparate groups as the General Federation of Women's Clubs and the Women's National Committee of the Socialist Party. On hand was the National Women's Trade Union League, and the United Daughters of the Confederacy sent greetings. Mrs. Pankhurst spoke briefly, and Emilie Todd Helm, widow of the Confederate general Ben Hardin Helm and half-sister of Mary Todd Lincoln, welcomed the suffragists.

As evidence of the new consciousness of women's groups that formerly were purely social, Patty Blackburn Semple, president of the Louisville Women's Club, told the convention:

> When the Women's Club was organized three subjects were tabooed—religion, politics and woman suffrage. We kept to the resolution for awhile but gradually we found that our efforts in behalf of civic improvements and the correcting of outrageous abuses

were handicapped at every turn by politics. Our club will be twenty-one years old in November, and—we want to vote!

With the support of socialites and socialists, union leaders and ex-Confederates, votes for women now seemed inevitable. Two years later, in 1913, 200 Louisville suffragists staged a parade, led by Mrs. John B. Castleman, the first public suffrage march in the South. Laura Clay did not approve of such bold tactics; she felt they might offend the public.

When suffrage came in 1920, Miss Clay did not share in the joy of ratification. In the last years an advocate of states' rights, she had resigned from the Kentucky ERA when Congress passed the federal amendment in 1919. From then on, she actually fought the amendment.

To many women in the South, "women's suffrage" meant "white women's suffrage." Kate Gordon of Louisiana was one of these. More moderate than the outspokenly racist Kate Gordon, Laura Clay was a white supremacist, as were many others of her day, and joined the states' rights forces. State action, rather than federal amendment, would permit Southern states to deal as they saw fit with the black woman voter. For Kentucky, with its small population of blacks, Miss Clay advocated an education requirement for women voters. This qualification would not refer to race, but in a practical sense, at that time it would have barred from the polls many more black than white women.

When ratification was pending in Tennessee, the final state needed to add the amendment to the Constitution, Laura Clay went to Nashville to fight her old suffrage allies. Carrie Chapman Catt, president of the NAWSA, wrote of the last-ditch lobbying she saw at first hand: "The opposition of every sort is here, fighting with no scruple, desperately. Women, including Kate Gordon and Laura Clay, are here appealing to Negrophobia and every other cave man's prejudice."

Laura Clay herself claimed that states' rights, not race, determined her position. But Sophonisba Breckinridge, legal scholar and a contemporary in suffrage work, wrote in 1921 of the issue: "The question of 'states' rights' in the decade 1910-1920, as in 1861, was really a question of the negro."

It seems a sad ending to a gallant fight. Laura Clay had contributed heavily to Kentucky women. When success was in the air, she may have felt passed over, deprived of her old authority in the movement. It was not that she had gotten weary. Indeed, she undertook in her remaining years—she lived to age ninety-two—to reform some of the bias against women in the Episcopal church, scope enough for her vast energy.

Closely allied with the early suffrage movement was the Women's Christian Temperance Union, led for years in Kentucky by Frances Beauchamp. In 1892, the state WCTU adopted a franchise department, believing that only through the ballot could they effectively challenge the alcohol problem. Laura Clay needed the WCTU, and she wrote that it "proved a faithful and valuable ally in educating public sentiment and obtaining desired legislation."

Possibly this alliance of temperance and suffrage workers attracted to suffrage the strong and well-financed opposition of the liquor industry. But the alliance was necessary: WCTU members were numerous and well-organized; suffragists, in the early going, were not. Moreover, both statewide and nationally, the distillers and brewers would have fought women's suffrage anyway, as did the meat-packers, the oil companies, the railroads, the city political machines, the Catholic church, and other powerful interests that feared change or reform.

Since the failure of prohibition, it has become more difficult to recognize the legitimacy of the temperance grievances against alcohol. Often the butt of jokes, these women, seen in the context of their times, were trying to solve real problems. Heavy drinking and violence were commonplace, and women with families were at the mercy, physically and economically, of the drinking breadwinner. A family might

The temperance movement in Kentucky was organized before the suffrage movement; they worked together.

Suffrage becomes fashionable: the 1916 Democratic convention

starve while Kentucky law allowed him to drink up his own earnings and those of his wife as well. The temperance solution, of course, was to abolish alcohol.

Theirs was an uphill fight. Kentucky had a reputation as a hard-drinking state. Liquor was a part of everyday living. For example, a Bourbon County church-women's group in 1881 compiled a cookbook containing a powerful remedy for dyspepsia: two ounces each of lady's-slipper root, balm of Gilead, and gum turpentine, an ounce of red percoon, and three pints of brandy. Those afflicted were advised to let the mixture stand for a few days and then take a little before each meal. Further, a remedy for horse colic—presumably also the responsibility of the housewife—called for both laudanum and whiskey.

In her memoirs, the Kentucky-born temperance crusader Carry Nation recalls that her father used to pass around an alcoholic mixture as a cure-all for relatives. The practice was not unusual; indeed, her father was the most normal member of the family.

Growing up in Garrard County, not far from the brick house built by the colorful Whitleys, Carry Amelia Moore had relatives who were most unusual. Even in a rural area tolerant of eccentrics, her maternal grandmother Campbell was considered insane. This grandmother stayed for years in her room, where she had given birth to ten children, three of them also insane and others somewhat odd. One of these, Carry Moore's aunt, is said to have thought now and again that she was a weathervane, and to have tried to climb to the housetop to pursue her vocation.

Carry Nation's mother, Mary Campbell Moore, started off modestly in her fantasies, announcing at first that she was a lady-in-waiting to Queen Victoria. After gaining experience in that capacity, she promoted herself to queen, wearing a cut-glass crown around the house and seeing members of the family by appointment only. Apparently undisturbed by his wife's fantasies, Carry Nation's father provided her mother with a plush-upholstered carriage, a small black boy to ride on the back as a footman, and a black man in a hunting jacket to ride ahead as an outrider, blowing a hunting horn to announce royal visits around the Kentucky countryside. Mrs. Nation recalled her excitement as a child when she was allowed to ride with the queen and her entourage, once sweeping majestically down the main street of Lancaster.

Years later, Carry Nation's own daughter, Charlien Gloyd, spent years in an insane asylum, much to the mother's grief. Carry Nation loved religion and hated drink, but Charlien did an about-face, developing a distaste for religion and "a great craving for stimulants which I had to guard her against."

In her autobiography, *The Use and Need of Carry A. Nation*, she looks back lovingly on the Kentucky years, first in Garrard County, then in 1851, when she was five, at a place two miles from Danville, and finally in 1854, on a farm between Midway and Versailles. In Woodford County the family was obviously well thought of, for her father served on the board of trustees in the building of the new orphans' home at Midway.

The family then moved West, where Carry Nation began to observe the effects of heavy drinking all around her in Kansas. Many misfits had drifted from the more orderly East to the rough frontier life, and violence often went along with drink. Not only were Carry Nation's neighbors victims of the miseries of alcohol, but her first husband was an alcoholic who died young.

Frequently joined by other women, Carry Nation began her self-styled "hatchetations," smashing saloons up and down the state of Kansas. As she smashed, she sang hymns, occasionally accompanied by a hand organ playing an entirely different hymn in the heat of the fray. She was often imprisoned, and cheerfully addressed judges as "Your Dishonor," a practice that probably added to the time she spent in jail.

In July of 1904, she returned to Kentucky to speak at Elizabethtown, which she describes unfeelingly as "one of those bad rum towns in Kentucky." There a saloonkeeper named G. R. Neighbors nearly killed her:

I passed this man and walking into his saloon, said: "Why are you in this business, drugging and robbing the people?" "You get out." I replied: "Yes you want a resptable [sic] woman to get out, but you will make any woman's boy a disgrace. You ought to be ashamed." I then passed out going to the hall. After the lecture I passed by his place again. He was sitting in a chair in front of his saloon, and I said, "Are you the man that runs this business?" and in a moment with an oath he picked up the chair and with all his strength sent it down with a crash on my head. I came near falling, caught myself, and he lifted the chair the second time, striking me over the back, the blood began to cover my face and run down from a cut on my forehead. I cried out, "He has killed me." An officer caught the chair to prevent the third blow. . . . Had it not been for my bonnet, I should have suffered more.

Although police saw the attack, they did not arrest Neighbors, a failure that incensed Mrs. Nation. The next morning, Mrs. Bettie James drove in from her farm two miles outside Elizabethtown and swore out a warrant for the saloonkeeper. But the trial was put off until November, when Carry Nation would be long gone, and other saloonkeepers went bond for the assailant.

Mrs. Nation had to spend most of a day in bed, highly unusual for her: she usually strapped a beefsteak on a blackened eye and trudged on to her next confrontation. That night she nearly fainted at her lecture but managed to finish. However, she concluded that there was hope for Elizabethtown: "there is a fine prohibition sentiment, and great indignation" at the attack upon her.

In her spare time, Mrs. Nation edited her own publications, *The Hatchet* and *The Smasher's Mail*, which often contained letters from Kentuckians. These were usually abusive, condemning her work or inviting her back to her home state to sample the new drink, the Carry Nation Cocktail. These letters she ran without editorial comment, in a column with the restrained title, "Letters from Hell."

Although the WCTU shared Carry Nation's goals, it was often embarrassed by her excesses. At times, she was sharp-tongued, witty, and highly effective in her cause. At other times, she seemed an authentic lunatic, accusing her enemies of pumping vile poison gas and viler cigarette smoke through the keyhole of her room. At her death, it was indicated that she suffered from congenital syphilis, a disease that would account for the family peculiarities.

Carry Nation's attempts to remove the symptoms, rather than the cause, of social ills seem bizarre in retrospect, her craving for martyrdom and her megalomania fantastic. She quotes with obvious pleasure in her autobiography a favorite song, written, she says, by some of her many admirers:

> Hurrah, Samantha, Mrs. Nation is in town!
> So get on your bonnet and your Sunday-meeting gown
> Oh, I am so blamed excited I am hopping up and down
> Hurrah, Samantha, Carry Nation is in town!

But her views were shared by thousands. She thought of herself as a conserver of values, a protector of home and family. At the outset of her autobiography, she writes: "I represent the distracted, suffering, loving motherhood of the world. Who, becoming aroused with a righteous fury rebelled at this torture." Thus the saloon-wrecking Kentuckian specifically identified herself with other women.

Close ties bound other reform movements to that of higher education for women. The Kentucky ERA had pursued higher education along with the vote, and the WCTU asked for, and got, an appropriation in 1900 for a women's dormitory at the state university in Lexington. Because 1900 was the year that Governor William Goebel was assassinated, the ERA stayed away from Frankfort as the better part of valor. But the WCTU was undeterred by the tumult and got the money for what would be Patterson Hall, which was not completed, however, until 1904.

Committed to equal education for equal minds, for decades Laura Clay urged the University of the South at Sewanee, Tennessee, to accept women. But it did not capitulate until 1969. In the later years of her life, she always attached a note to her annual contribution to the Episcopal church, stipulating that "None of this is to go to Sewanee."

An institution that did not delay coeducation was the future University of Kentucky, then named the Agricultural and Mechanical College of Kentucky and called "State College." Early in its existence, in 1880, within a decade of its actually getting under way, Judge W. B. Kinkead pushed coeducation through the doubtful board of trustees. The argument was that the college now had a normal school for teacher training, that many teachers were women, and that it would be unreasonable to keep women out.

The male students at State College were all military cadets and a rough-hewn lot, but they seem not to have objected to the entrance of women. The first woman did not graduate from the college itself until 1888, and the event called forth a poem from a newspaper contributor:

> Sweet fruit of this collegiate tree that burst
> Into fresh maiden blossom here today,
> Among these awkward boys, like smiling May,
> Making the cold earth glorious. I hail
> With joy the first most fair, most learned female.

Less ecstatic over learned females was cross-town Kentucky University (later rechristened with its original name, Transylvania). All male since its founding in 1780, the college was inclined to stay that way. Laura Clay and the ERA were determined that it should not. Collecting signatures on petitions, the ERA took these documents to the board of curators. The college president, C. L. Loos, favored coeducation, and after some study, the curators agreed. More than fifty years after Oberlin College in Ohio had admitted women, Transylvania opened its doors to them in 1889. For years, women students roomed in town, but they had their own separate dining room, supervised by a matron. Julia Cassandra Mathis, in 1894 the first woman graduated from a four-year course, had to sit on the back row of every class she took. She was also required to have a chaperone accompany her to the classroom, although at five feet ten and 175 pounds, she seemed able to look after herself.

Berea College admitted women from its start, in 1855, because of its unusual evolution. The college had gradually developed from a secondary school, which had taught both girls and boys. In 1892, Georgetown College and Wesleyan in Winchester decided to admit women. Last of all was Centre College in Danville. A men's college until 1926, it then merged with Kentucky College for Women, also in Danville, in a form of coordinate education. In 1961, women's residence halls were built on the Centre campus itself.

At the Law Department of the University of Louisville, the class of 1892 objected to women students, claiming that "nice girls would not want to study law." They also felt that women would inhibit their manly, and off-color, habits of speech in the classroom. When several young women from Anchorage applied for admission, men students were alarmed. Learning that the women would have to attend class early in the afternoon to get back to Anchorage by nightfall, the men voted to hold the advanced class first each afternoon. Thus they preserved the law school as a male sanctuary for the time being.

But women students came to college in gradually increasing numbers, and a few entered careers that would earlier have been closed to them. For example, a State College graduate of 1890, Margaret Agnes Wilson, reported that she was a chemist in Deadwood, Colorado; Margaret Ingels, who graduated from U.K. in 1916, was the country's first woman mechanical engineer; and Sarah Blanding (U.K., 1923) became president of Vassar College.

Like men students, the new women undergraduates obviously relished the fun of college life as well as its intellectual pleasures. Chafing-dish feasts at night and women's

111

basketball were popular. A *Kentuckian* of 1904 reports a game as "one vast tide of straight hair, stray hair, curls and ribbons reversed and cries of 'Here, Rebekah,' and 'Oh, Gemima, how could you?' " Transylvania women players complained that the basketball sometimes hit the gaslights in the gymnasium. But it was all fun. Men students at State College were not allowed to watch these games, but in 1904, women players took a male student, dressed in women's clothes, to Georgetown. His disguise was not penetrated until too late, after he had seen the forbidden spectacle. His punishment was a problem. Although the college had no fewer than 180 rules of conduct, there was no rule against dressing up as a coed. He got off with a general reprimand, and the women apparently went unpunished.

Hedged about by regulations and watched by matrons as they were, these women students experienced a freedom their mothers never knew. It should be no surprise that they would no longer be willing to accept the legal and social restrictions that limited women's lives.

Certainly, they did not collapse with brain fever and physical breakdowns, as opponents of higher education for women had predicted. In Sunday sermons and in articles by physicians, dire consequences were foretold for college women. And women who wanted to attend professional schools, like the Anchorage women, evoked far more hostility than did prospective undergraduates.

In Louisville, at the late date of 1923, a Baptist publishing house put out a collection of essays by Baptist ministers, voicing typical arguments against the higher education of women.

"Menstruation," wrote the Reverend J. W. Porter, "is of itself, quite sufficient to produce mental peculiarities." The Louisville minister then quoted a so-called authority of the previous century, Dr. Clouston, on this subject and concluded with his own opinions, shared by many:

It is for this and other reasons that many have been led to doubt the wisdom of co-education. At such a time neither mind nor body

A rural Kentucky
schoolteacher

A dorm party at Georgetown College

should be subjected to exacting labor. In Europe, the contracts for singers often contain provision for rest during the monthly period.

After observing that the president of Bryn Mawr, the distinguished M. Carey Thomas, "is about as well fitted to educate young women, as a saloonkeeper is to administer the Lord's supper," the Reverend Porter added a cautionary note to young women: "It is a sad and sickening fact, that a majority of the female graduates of many of our universities never marry. In light of the view they are taught to hold concerning the sanctity of marriage, their single blessedness may probably prove a real blessing to the men they might have married." With ten other Baptist spokesmen, the Reverend Porter decried feminism, the vote for women, careers, and birth control—all as products of anarchy and Bolshevism. He warned the Kentucky citizenry: "The furies stand upon the battlements lashing the credulous to frenzy. The wanton girls of the he-girl schools would abolish the Home. The wanton women in the band-wagons would abolish religion [as] in France during the Terror."

It is interesting that the ministers, physicians, and other pundits so concerned for the health of college women were not worried about the health of factory women or farm tenant women. The real threat in higher education lay in the chance that women might become autonomous.

As educated women began to organize themselves, many turned to the conditions of the urban poor. Far from the tide of immigrants and the growth of heavy industrialization, Kentucky women nonetheless felt the influence of the settlement-house movement. Evidence of concern for the urban poor is clear in a law passed by the Kentucky legislature in 1898—introduced at the urging of Louisville women—to provide for police matrons. To assure the good character of these matrons, the act stipulated that no woman be appointed without the recommendation of a committee made up of one woman chosen by each of these Louisville organizations: the Home of Friendless Women, the Flower

Mission, the Free Kindergarten Association, the Humane Society, the Charity Organization Society, the City Federation of Women's Clubs, the Kentucky Children's Home Society, the WCTU, and the Women's Christian Association—a fair number of social service organizations for 1898. Settlement houses themselves, like Neighborhood House and Cabbage Patch, were established early in Louisville, where well-informed women knew of the work of Jane Addams, Sophonisba Breckinridge, and others in Chicago.

Sophonisba Breckinridge, a brilliant pioneer in social work, was a Lexington woman, born in 1866 into a distinguished Kentucky family. After reading law and becoming the first woman accepted by the Kentucky bar, she tried to practice in Lexington, but clients were few. Casting about for some use to make of her life, she went to the University of Chicago, where she earned a J.D. degree in law and a Ph.D. in political science. After serving as dean and director of research at the Chicago School of Civics and Philanthropy, she eventually achieved that school's merger with the University of Chicago, as the University's Graduate School of Social Service Administration. Later she was president of the American Association of Schools of Social Work.

Establishing rigorous academic standards for social workers, she was largely responsible for making social work a profession—and during the New Deal years, that profession came into its own. Many reform efforts claimed her energy: the investigation of factory conditions for women and children, investigations of tenement conditions, the establishment of juvenile court systems, the study of the effects of poverty on family life, the advancement of the rights of immigrants, of blacks, and of women. A sister-in-law of Madeline McDowell Breckinridge, whose biography she wrote, Sophonisba Breckinridge was a woman of charm and warmth with strong ties to Kentucky.

Not only did the settlement-house movement affect those concerned about city slums, but it also had an impact on those with a new interest—the Kentucky mountains. A fertile field for scholar and social worker, the mountains offered romantic scenery, unlike the city slum, and a sense of adventure without real danger to the traveler. Outsiders began to drive buggies, and later, their high-axled cars, over rudimentary roads, or they rode horseback, fording creeks and camping out at night. Long isolated, mountain people had genuine needs, especially in health and education, and many of the reforms undertaken in Eastern Kentucky were initiated by women.

To the Kentucky Federation of Women's Clubs in 1899 came a letter from a Hazard minister, asking if the federation would send someone to teach women in his area about proper diet, cooking, sewing, and child care. Katharine Pettit of Lexington, active in the WCTU and the Federation of Women's Clubs, had traveled in Eastern Kentucky and knew of the poverty there and the hard lives that women led. The challenge attracted her. She carried the settlement-house concept to the mountains, founding first the Hindman Settlement School and later the Pine Mountain Settlement School.

She also interested her friend, Linda Neville of Lexington, in this work. In 1907, Miss Neville began her lifelong work of combating blindness. Trachoma was a prevalent disease in the mountains, and mountain people had no access to treatment. Persuading more than 3,000 of them to accompany her to Lexington over the years, Miss Neville also convinced city physicians to hold clinics in Eastern Kentucky.

Perhaps the best known of the women reformers in the Kentucky mountains is Mary Breckinridge, founder in 1925 of the famous Frontier Nursing Service in Hyden. Educated at European schools, Mary Breckinridge, a cousin of Sophonisba Breckinridge, faced the problem experienced by other intelligent, vigorous, well-to-do women who found their traditional roles vapid. When she was widowed young, Mary Breckinridge turned to the study of nursing. Later, after the deaths of two children and the dissolution of a second marriage, she trained in a British hospital to become a certified midwife.

Linda Neville and two of her nurses aid the blind in Eastern Kentucky

A traveling midwife from Mary Breckinridge's Frontier Nursing Service

Mary Breckinridge decided that she could best put her life to use by establishing a midwife service in Leslie County, a county that had no doctors. The area had both a high birth rate and an appalling record of maternal and infant deaths. Soon she expanded her goals to include health care for entire families.

Between 1925 and 1955, the FNS delivered 12,262 babies and inoculated 213,906 persons, Mrs. Breckinridge reported with pride. In an era when the maternal death rate for white women in the United States was 34 per 10,000 live births (it was worse for black women), the FNS death rate was only 9.1.

Not the least of Mary Breckinridge's gifts was her flair for public relations. Those who heard her speak recall her eloquent, personal style as remarkable. Florence Shelby Cantrill, who heard all of Kentucky's women reformers speak, considered Mary Breckinridge the best of all. Mrs. Breckinridge also possessed a rare gift for writing, and her autobiography, *Wide Neighborhoods*, memorably tells her own story and that of the Frontier Nursing Service.

Mrs. Breckinridge astutely maintained contacts all over the country, and years after the advent to the mountains of electricity, telephones, automobiles, and interstate highways, affluent young women were still being sent to Wendover to spend the summer as horseback "couriers" for the well-publicized FNS. When she died in 1965 at age eighty-four, Mary Breckinridge had raised an astonishing six million dollars for her medical phenomenon.

Another woman who was drawn to the mountains was Alice Lloyd of Boston, who arrived in Knott County with her mother in 1916. Aged forty at the time, Alice Lloyd apparently came with no definite plans except the wish to do something constructive with her life. She stayed forty-six years, channeling her energies into education for isolated young people. With volunteer help and donated money, she built 100 elementary and secondary schools, all eventually taken over by county systems. She then concentrated on

Caney Creek Junior College, which she founded in 1923 at Pippa Passes, a name she took from Browning. As at well-established Berea College, tuition was free, but students had to work, and they had to have a serious sense of purpose. For thirty-nine years she ran the junior college with an iron hand.

A Radcliffe graduate and a former writer for a Boston newspaper, Alice Lloyd kept up her contacts in the East to good effect. Not only did she build her schools with volunteer help, she also staffed them with volunteer faculties, often graduates of famous Eastern universities who taught for the experience. A tireless writer of solicitations, Alice Lloyd raised two and one-half million dollars for Caney Creek, later renamed in her honor.

A young native of Eastern Kentucky also took an active role in education in the mountains. She was Cora Wilson, later Cora Wilson Stewart, who at age twenty began teaching in her home county, Rowan, boarding in country homes. In 1901, when she was twenty-six, she was elected superintendent of county schools. Reelected in 1909, she was elected in 1911 the first woman president of the Kentucky Education Association.

Although the teaching profession employed mostly women, it ordinarily offered positions of authority to men only. Yet Mrs. Stewart rose rapidly, acquiring considerable renown for her "Moonlight Schools," night schools held on moonlit nights for adult illiterates. Spreading the word by schoolchildren, the Rowan teachers enrolled 1,200 adults in 1911 and 1,600 in 1912.

Mrs. Stewart wrote simple texts for adults that would not insult them and at the same time would provide some useful information. So successful was the enterprise that she began to take news of her work to other counties and states, and she became nationally recognized.

The beauty of these schools for adults, it was said, was that they cost nothing. No donations had to be raised, no tax money used. The "Moonlight Schools" were subsidized, however, by the unpaid work of county teachers, who taught during the day and returned to school at night to teach adults for no additional pay.

Although promoters of worthy causes in the Kentucky mountains often praised the prolific quality of the mountain people, it occurred to some reformers that bearing and rearing a dozen or more children in a poverty-ridden county had its drawbacks. Photographs, taken in Eastern Kentucky, of a family group of thirty-seven close relatives might delight those spectators who feared—as many authorities did—that small families of "Anglo-Saxon stock" were being outnumbered by large immigrant families, a trend that would result in "racial suicide." But bringing up a dozen children in poverty is not a spectator sport. To mountain people who quoted the biblical "be fruitful and multiply," the Reverend Robert Sparrow, a volunteer in the birth-control movement, always responded that "the Bible didn't mean for one couple to do it all."

Birth control was being practiced before World War I by well-informed women who had money to go to private physicians. But it was decades before such information reached the mountains.

In 1936, a group of Berea women attended a conference of the Council of the Southern Mountains, held in West Virginia, and when they returned to Berea they formed what would become the Mountain Maternal Health League. They learned that Dr. Clarence Gamble, a Philadelphia philanthropist and researcher in contraception, would pay the salary of a nurse and furnish her a car. In return, the organization must keep careful case records. The Berea women accepted, and an arrangement began that lasted until 1943.

The first nurse for the league was Lena Gilliam, who was born in a two-room log cabin on the Rockcastle River. To help her mother with the growing family, she had given up a scholarship to Annville Institute. In her eleventh childbirth, the mother died, leaving the sixteen-year-old girl to

Rural mother of twelve

One of Cora Wilson Stewart's "Moonlight Schools" for adult illiterates

bring up the ten younger children. Eventually, Lena Gilliam got the chance to go to nursing school, and she became a dedicated advocate of birth control. On behalf of the Mountain Maternal Health League, she visited 500 families in the first year and a half, traveling over Madison, Jackson, and Rockcastle counties. In these homes, her information was received with appreciation, as letters to the league at this time attest.

When Dr. Louise Hutchins and her husband arrived at Berea in 1939, she immediately became interested in the league's work. Born in China of missionary parents, she had practiced medicine there and was a resourceful leader. When Dr. Gamble's research ended in 1943—he concluded that contraceptive jelly was 85 percent effective—Dr. Hutchins had to finance the league's work from donations. Of the years that followed, Dr. Hutchins said: "Our funds grew slim—too slim to even pay a nurse to keep up the field work. These were truly hard times."

Since they could not send a nurse out, Dr. Hutchins established a clinic at Berea Hospital, hoping that women would come to it, and many did. Working on a meager budget, she recruited midwife nurses—graduates of the Frontier Nursing Service—persuaded sympathetic county health nurses to distribute "bootleg" birth-control information and supplies, and got grants from the Association for Voluntary Sterilization for tubal ligations and vasectomies.

Sterilizations have been condemned by some ethnic groups, among them some Puerto Ricans in New York City, who claim that such surgery is a means of population engineering, and worse, a tactic not fully understood by the patients themselves. But this criticism does not apply to the work of the Mountain Maternal Health League, Dr. Hutchins maintained. "Women with large families welcomed tubal ligations, especially when the new and simpler laproscopic method came in. We met with no resistance. Only on the rarest occasion did we find a woman who said it was the Lord's will to continue giving birth," she said.

China, her birthplace, contributed much to Dr. Hutchins's beliefs about women and childbirth. "In China I saw women who had twelve children and they all died," she said. "In Eastern Kentucky I saw women who had twelve children and they all lived. But they lived in two rooms in the barest circumstances."

Returning to the Orient, Dr. Hutchins spent three years, from 1967 to 1970, in Hong Kong, learning to work with intrauterine devices. Back in Kentucky, from 1971 through 1978, she treated 41,572 mountain women. At age 68, in 1979, she continued to go out daily as a clinician for the Kentucky Department of Health, distributing contraceptive supplies and information. Still driven by the thought of more work to be done, she spoke of "a crying need for money, even today. We have about two hundred women in the mountain area who want ligations right now, yet, for example, we are allowed money for only one tubing and one vasectomy a year in Madison County." For Dr. Hutchins, the birth-control struggle had not ended.

The birth-control movement in Kentucky, however, did not start in the mountains. The woman who pioneered the movement in the state was Jean Brandeis, later Jean Brandeis Tachau, of Louisville. From a family with an active social conscience—Supreme Court Justice Louis Brandeis was her uncle—she had worked with the Children's Protective Association in Louisville after World War I. In this work she saw families with more children than they could care for, and she tried to get some established organization to support the cause of birth control. But all the groups that she approached felt that the issue was too controversial. It was also regarded by many as indelicate. Considerable personal courage was required to launch the birth-control movement in Kentucky.

By 1933, Mrs. Tachau had organized a group of fifty-one, including thirteen physicians and one minister. The others were Louisville women willing to be identified with the issue. In the spring, the group held the first Kentucky Birth Control Conference, and by summer of 1933, they had organized the Kentucky Birth Control League.

After some difficulty, Mrs. Tachau persuaded Norton Infirmary to open a weekly clinic. At that time, black people were barred from Norton, and to reach these people and others, the league opened clinics at Cabbage Patch Settlement and Trinity Mission. The Louisville Maternal Health Clinic was formed as a branch of the Kentucky Birth Control League, and in 1938 opened offices on Floyd Street, with Dr. Esther Wallner serving as clinician.

While these efforts went on in Louisville, the Kentucky Birth Control League was expanding its work into other counties. In the mountains, the league used the Health House of Line Fork Cabin—an extension of the Pine Mountain Settlement School—as a base of operations for Lutrella Baker, a practical nurse. Thus both the Louisville-based organization and the Mountain Maternal Health League were operating in different parts of the mountains.

At that time, possible contraceptives for women's use included jelly, foam powder, diaphragm, and sponge. From pharmaceutical companies, Mrs. Tachau arranged to get free supplies in exchange for records of the effectiveness of each method.

Kentucky women who wanted some means of birth control often wrote the Louisville office for help. One letter, for example, said: "I am already a mother of ten boys ranging from one to fifteen years. Please help me for my health is very bad." Said another: "I have been married eleven years, have had ten conceptions in that time and I am pregnant now. Our home is a wreck."

But contraception was still controversial to many. When the Louisville *Courier-Journal* devoted a full page to birth control in 1941 and supported the movement editorially, the paper was threatened with boycotts and cancelled subscriptions. Moreover, the Jefferson County grand jury condemned the *Courier*, claiming that the paper had issued "an invitation to abortion." In time, the storm blew over. "We started early," Mrs. Tachau recalled. "We were a pioneering effort in the state and thus ran into opposition."

In Lexington, no opposition developed. There the prime

mover behind birth control was Laura Kinkead Walton. In the fall of 1935, she called a group of friends to a meeting at her house, and they agreed to support a birth-control clinic. Miss Lake Johnson of Good Samaritan Hospital gave the group houseroom, and in early 1936 they opened a clinic with $250 and without fanfare.

"We didn't exactly wave a flag about what we were doing," Mrs. Walton said. With the support of three women doctors—Dr. Josephine Hunt, Dr. Caroline Scott, and Dr. Emily Warfield—the clinic attracted women mostly by word of mouth. To undermine possible criticism that Planned Parenthood was anti-family, Mrs. Walton got as many pregnant volunteers as she could to work at the clinic.

But she attributed the lack of opposition in Lexington less to general acceptance than to its low profile and the prominence of its supporters. Mrs. Walton's father, Judge W. B. Kinkead—the same man who convinced other trustees at State College to admit women students—was a powerful figure in Lexington, and local politicians were wary of attacking his daughter or an agency that had his tacit support.

A forthright woman, Mrs. Walton did not worry about objections. Her interest in birth control led her to travel to Arizona to meet with Margaret Sanger, birth-control leader who was then working with Mexican-American women. Recalling those years, Mrs. Walton was pleased by the thought that in a strictly segregated era, the Lexington clinic served both black and white women. To her mind, the birth-control movement had its basis in a simple concept of equity. As she and her friends felt, "If we had it, the poor should have it. It had to come for the sake of justice."

What part did the state of Kentucky play in the birth-control movement? None. Margaret Sanger had begun her work in 1912, and contraception was widely available to the well-to-do. But not until 1962, fifty years later, did the Kentucky Department of Health permit county health departments to provide contraceptive information and supplies.

And why the state's reluctance? Dr. Hutchins maintained that the reason lay not in any organized pressure but in the politicians' fear that such pressure would come, principally from the large Catholic voting bloc in Louisville, where the state Department of Health was located for many years. "In fact, we noticed a big difference when the department was moved from Louisville to Frankfort," Dr. Hutchins said. Opposition to birth control from fundamentalist religions was negligible, she added. It was the Catholics' voting power that frightened Kentucky politicians—hence Mrs. Tachau's difficulties in Louisville.

Support and opposition to the birth-control movement did not always follow stereotypical religious lines, Dr. Hutchins observed. Interestingly, a physician who headed the maternal and child health services in Kentucky "wouldn't touch us with a ten-foot pole—and she was Protestant. On the other hand, a Catholic physician was very supportive," she said. Moreover, the major breakthrough in federal funds came during the administrations of a Catholic president, John F. Kennedy, and his successor, Lyndon Johnson. And federal funds made all the difference.

Political expediency, rather than religious ideology, lay at the heart of Kentucky's refusal to educate the poor in birth control. Nor did the medical establishment push the matter. Not until 1967 was any official reference to contraception made at meetings of the Kentucky Medical Association, Dr. Hutchins noted, and that came in a speech she herself gave. Generations were born and grew up, while Kentucky women who could not afford private physicians depended on women volunteers, working on donated money, for information essential to women's lives.

Remarkable women have lived in Kentucky from the start, and none more remarkable than the women reformers. Some were once considered radical; others have been written off as "ladies bountiful," imposing their middle-class values on their beneficiaries. Yet to the powerless, to whom society and its institutions offered only indifference, these women reformers gave years of their lives. Most notably, they gave to other women.

That the status of women is still ambiguous might not have surprised them. With her usual prescience, Emmeline Pankhurst warned Kentucky women in 1920 not to "give up the fight" as soon as they got the vote. Apparently many did, thus setting the stage for another upsurge of feminism and anti-feminism in the last decades of the twentieth century, as once again, society tried to define the aspirations of half the population.

Principal Sources

Chapter 1

Standard histories of Kentucky provide background but little information about women. More useful are Robert L. Kincaid, *Wilderness Road* (New York: Bobbs-Merrill, 1947) and Harriette Simpson Arnow, *Seedtime on the Cumberland* (New York: Macmillan, 1960). Anecdotes about women appear in John Alexander M'Clung, *Sketches of Western Adventures* (Cincinnati: U. P. James, 1839); Charles Gano Talbert, *Benjamin Logan: Kentucky Frontiersman* (Lexington: University of Kentucky Press, 1962); George W. Ranck, *The Traveling Church* ([n.p.], 1910) and *Boonesborough: Its Founding, Pioneer Struggles, Indian Experiences, Transylvania Days and Revolutionary Annals* (Louisville: J. P. Morton, 1901); and Louise P. Kellogg, "A Kentucky Pioneer Tells Her Story of Early Boonesborough and Harrodsburg," *Filson Club Quarterly* 3 (1929): 223-36. The novel *The Great Meadow*, by Elizabeth Madox Roberts, is well researched.

Chapter 2

An account of Jenny Wiley is provided by William Elsey Connelley, *Eastern Kentucky Papers: The Founding of Harman's Station, with an account of the Indian Captivity of Mrs. Jennie Wiley and the Explorations and Settlement of the Big Sandy Valley in the Virginias and Kentucky* (New York: Torch Press, 1910). M'Clung also refers to captives. References to Indian women are based on Arnow, M'Clung, and on Wilbur R. Jacobs (ed.), *The Appalachian Indian*

Frontier: The Edmond Atkin Report and Plan of 1755 (Columbia: University of South Carolina Press, 1954).

Chapter 3

The rural woman's life is described by Daniel Drake, *Pioneer Life in Kentucky, 1785-1800*, Emmet Field Horine (ed.), (New York: Henry Schumann, 1948). A prominent woman's life is depicted in the unpublished letters of Margaretta Brown of "Liberty Hall," Frankfort. Other sources are Clement Eaton, *Henry Clay and the Art of American Politics* (Boston: Little, Brown, 1957); Rebecca Smith Lee, *Mary Austin Holley* (Austin: University of Texas Press, 1962); Richard C. Wade, *The Urban Frontier: Pioneer Life in Early Pittsburgh, Cincinnati, Lexington, Louisville, and St. Louis* (Chicago: University of Chicago Press, 1964); Edward Deming Andrews, *The People Called Shakers* (Oxford: Oxford University Press, 1953); Virginia Tatnall Peacock, *Famous American Belles of the Nineteenth Century* (Philadelphia: J. B. Lippincott, 1901); Ben J. Webb, *The Centenary of Catholicity in Kentucky* (Louisville: Charles A. Rodgers, 1884); Sister Mary Ramona Mattingly, *The Catholic Church on the Kentucky Frontier (1785-1812)*, (Washington, D.C.: The Catholic University of America, 1936); Ann Douglas, *The Feminization of American Culture* (New York: Knopf, 1977).

Chapter 4

Sources for slavery include Herbert G. Gutman, *The Black Family in Slavery and Freedom, 1750-1925* (New York: Pantheon Books, 1976); John W. Blassingame, *The Slave Community: Plantation Life in the Antebellum South* (New York: Oxford University Press, 1972); Boynton Merrill, Jr., *Jefferson's Nephews: A Frontier Tragedy* (Princeton: Princeton University Press, 1976); J. Winston Coleman, Jr., *Slavery Times in Kentucky* (Chapel Hill: University of North Carolina Press, 1940); Steven A. Channing,

Kentucky: A Bicentennial History (New York: Norton, 1977); *Five Slave Narratives: A Compendium* (New York: Arno Press and *New York Times*, 1968); Carter G. Woodson (ed.), *Free Negro Owners of Slaves in the U.S. in 1830* (New York: Negro Universities Press, 1968); and U.S. Works Projects Administration, "Slave Narratives: A Folk History of Slavery in the U.S. from Interviews with Former Slaves" (Washington, D.C.: Library of Congress film, 1941), Reel 7, "Kentucky."

Diaries of Kentucky women include G. Glenn Clift (ed.), *The Private War of Lizzie Hardin* (Frankfort: Kentucky Historical Society, 1963); John David Smith and William Cooper, Jr. (eds.), *Window on the War: Frances Dallam Peter's Lexington Civil War Diary* (Lexington: Lexington-Fayette County Historic Commission, 1976); and an unpublished account of a battle at Frankfort, Brown papers, "Liberty Hall," Frankfort.

Other sources are William H. Townsend, *Lincoln and His Wife's Home Town* (New York: Bobbs-Merrill, 1929); Ishbel Ross, *The President's Wife: Mary Todd Lincoln: A Biography* (New York: G. P. Putnam's Sons, 1973); Frank Moore, *Women of the War: Their Heroism and Self-Sacrifice* (Hartford, Conn.: S. S. Scranton, 1866); Mrs. W. T. Fowler, "Confederate Heroines: Mrs. Emily Thomas Tubman—Kentucky," *The United Daughters of the Confederacy Magazine* 25, no. 8 (August 1962): 14; Ruth Davenport Deiss, "Henrietta Hunt Morgan," *The United Daughters of the Confederacy Magazine* 25, no. 6 (June 1962): 15; and Edward T. James, Janet Wilson James, and Paul S. Boyer (eds.), *Notable American Women, 1607-1950* (Cambridge, Mass.: Harvard University Press, 1971).

Chapter 5

General background on working-class women in America appears in Barbara Mayer Wertheimer, *We Were There: The Story of Working Women in America* (New York: Pantheon Books, 1977), and Eleanor Flexner, *A Century of*

Struggle: The Women's Rights Movement in the United States (New York: Atheneum, 1972). Older works include Edith Abbott, *Women in Industry: A Study in American Economic History* (New York: D. Appleton and Co., 1915); U.S. Bureau of Labor, *Report on Condition of Woman and Child Wage-Earners in the United States*, 19 vols., 1910-13.

For labor in Kentucky, C. Herbert Finch, "Organized Labor in Louisville, 1885-1900" (unpublished dissertation, University of Kentucky, 1965) provides good background, although little information about women. The best sources are *Report of the Commission to Investigate the Conditions of Working Women in Kentucky* ([n.p.], December 1911); U.S. Department of Labor Women's Bureau, Bulletin No. 29, *Women in Kentucky Industries: A Study of Hours, Wages, and Working Conditions* (1923); Bulletin No. 162, *Women in Kentucky Industries: 1937* (1938).

Other sources are Paul E. Fuller, *Laura Clay and the Woman's Rights Movement* (Lexington: University Press of Kentucky, 1975); Edith Summers Kelley, *Weeds* (Lost American Fiction Series, Carbondale: Southern Illinois University Press, 1972); interview with Ira Massie; files of *The Transylvanian*.

Chapter 6

An essential source is Elizabeth Cady Stanton, Susan B. Anthony, Mathilda Gage, and Ida Husted Harper (eds.), *The History of Woman Suffrage*, 6 vols. (Rochester, N.Y.: 1881-1922). Other background sources are Flexner; Aileen Kraditor, *The Ideas of the Woman Suffrage Movement: 1890-1920* (New York: Columbia University Press, 1965); Midge McKenzie, *Shoulder to Shoulder: A Documentary* (New York: Knopf, 1975); Trevor Lloyd, *Suffragettes International* (New York: American Heritage Press, 1971); William L. O'Neill, *Divorce in the Progressive Era* (New Haven: Yale University Press, 1971); Suzanne D. Lebsock, "Radical Reconstruction and the Property Rights of Southern Women," *The Journal of Southern History* 43, no. 2

(May 1977): 195-216; Anne Firor Scott, *The Southern Lady: From Pedestal to Politics, 1830-1930* (Chicago: University of Chicago Press, 1970); Christopher Lasch, *The New Radicalism in America, 1889-1963: The Intellectual as a Social Type* (New York: Knopf, 1965); Linda Gordon, *Woman's Body, Woman's Right: A Social History of Birth Control in America* (New York: Grossman-Viking Press, 1976); James Reed, *From Private Vice to Public Virtue: The Birth Control Movement and American Society since 1830* (New York: Basic Books, 1978); Carroll Smith-Rosenberg and Charles Rosenberg, "The Female Animal: Medical and Biological Views of Woman and Her Role in Nineteenth-Century America," *Journal of American History* 60, no. 2 (September 1973): 332-56.

For Kentucky women, sources include Fuller's *Laura Clay;* Carry A. Nation, *The Use and Need of Carry A. Nation* (Topeka, Kansas: F. M. Steves, c. 1908 or 1909); Herbert Asbury, *Carry Nation* (New York: Knopf, 1929); Robert Lewis Taylor, *Vessel of Wrath: The Life and Times of Carry Nation* (New York: New American Library, 1968); Sophonisba Preston Breckinridge, *Madeline McDowell Breckinridge: A Leader in the New South* (Chicago: University of Chicago Press, 1921); Mary Breckinridge, *Wide Neighborhoods: A Story of the Frontier Nursing Service* (New York: Harper and Brothers, 1952); Cora Wilson Stewart, *Moonlight Schools: For the Emancipation of Adult Illiterates* (New York: E. P. Dutton, 1922); Willie Everette Nelms, Jr., "Cora Wilson Stewart: Crusader against Illiteracy" (unpublished master's thesis, University of Kentucky, 1973); Caroline Bird, *Enterprising Women* (New York: W. W. Norton, 1976); James F. Hopkins, *The University of Kentucky: Origins and Early Years* (Lexington: University of Kentucky Press, 1951); Frank L. McVey, *The Gates Open Slowly: A History of Education in Kentucky* (Lexington: University of Kentucky Press, 1949); Helen Deiss Irvin, *Hail Kentucky! A Pictorial History of the University of Kentucky* (Lexington: University of Kentucky Press, 1965); Kentucky Writers' Project, *A Centennial History of the University of*

Louisville (Louisville: American Guide Series, 1939); Elisabeth S. Peck, *Berea's First Century: 1855-1955* (Lexington: University of Kentucky Press, 1955); John D. Wright, Jr., *Transylvania: Tutor to the West* (Lexington: Transylvania University, 1975); John William Porter, *Feminism: Woman and Her Work* (Louisville: Baptist Book Concern, 1923); Elizabeth M. Cosby, *Family Planning in Kentucky: A History* ([n.p.], 1973). Information was also obtained from Arthur Flandreau, head librarian, Berea College, and John May, head librarian, Centre College, and from interviews with Florence Shelby Cantrill, Lexington; Jean Brandeis Tachau, Louisville; Laura Kinkead Walton, Lexington; and Dr. Louise Gilman Hutchins, of the Mountain Maternal Health League and the Kentucky Department of Health. *Notable American Women* was again valuable, as were the files of *The Kentuckian*, the *Kentucky University Bulletin*, the Louisville *Courier-Journal*, and the Lexington *Herald*.